Patti and her partner Pity

One little piece of peace

rney gets a hair raising lesson

The pan and the brush

SO THIS IS PEACE

by

Bob Hope

PICTURES BY LEW GLANZMAN, PUBLISHED
BY THE HOPE CORPORATION AND DISTRIBUTED
BY SIMON AND SCHUSTER

ALL RIGHTS RESERVED
INCLUDING THE RIGHT OF REPRODUCTION
IN WHOLE OR IN PART IN ANY FORM
COPYRIGHT, 1946, BY THE HOPE CORPORATION
PUBLISHED BY THE HOPE CORPORATION
DISTRIBUTED BY SIMON AND SCHUSTER, INC.
ROCKEFELLER CENTER, 1230 SIXTH AVENUE
NEW YORK 20, N. Y.

SECOND PRINTING

MANUFACTURED IN THE UNITED STATES OF AMERICA
BY AMERICAN BOOK–STRATFORD PRESS, INC., NEW YORK

This book about peace is respectfully dedicated to those who say, "I don't want to hear any more about the war." Remember that what you don't hear about, you forget. And when you forget what war's like . . . you're in danger.

B. H.

NOTE

Please forgive references to the European and Pacific Theaters of Operation. They may be the last of their kind any actor gets to make. The next war won't last long enough for us to get packed.

THE AUTHOR

PREFACE

IN SPITE *of the fact that half the nations of the world claimed to be fighting to sign a peace treaty, the end of the war came so suddenly that they were all caught with their pens down.*

Seven million servicemen suddenly found out that civilians were people, too. And what surprised them even more—that they were civilians.

But those guys soon discovered they couldn't duck me just by changing their suits and going home. During four years of war I went to every corner of the world—looking for a corner to hide in. And every place I went I met guys with dreams of how to enjoy a home they once took for granted. I had to see how they cashed those dreams.

So on the second anniversary of D-Day we established a small beachhead at Spokane, Washington, and started crisscrossing the country . . . double-crossing the audiences. And what pleased us most was that the guys showed up, just the way they did when they were in the Army. Only this time they had to pay. Except for that little detail it was the same show. We even traveled by air, just the way we did when we played for the Army . . . only this time we had to pay.

But it was a thrill being the first airborne vaudeville unit to attack undefended American cities. And in every one of them we met old friends. Only this time it was different. We used to meet a guy in a hospital on Guam who told us he was from Bridgeport and said, meet my buddy. Today we meet a

Preface

guy in Bridgeport who tells us he's from a hospital on Guam and says, meet the wife and kid.

And it's those kids that make you realize the peace must never again be broken.

You're even surer of this every time you come across some boy you saw in Europe or the Pacific, when he was a hale and hearty youngster with a big American grin, and you find him sitting in a wheel chair. Those guys smile . . . but their eyes and their gray hair make you understand that the GI Bill of Rights just can't solve all of war's wrongs.

Let's not kid ourselves: there are plenty of detours for some on that old Road to Utopia that runs between One War and One World. But the road from USO to UNO wasn't too tough for you-know-who. And you know why. War or peace, a moving target is toughest to hit. So I stayed packed. And copped a gander at One Nation as it began to realize that the atom had changed from the tiniest thing in a mighty world to the mightiest thing in a tiny world. And people saw in the newsreels that the two words "atomic bomb" were just the shortest way of saying "Where is everybody?"

Which adds up to this. Those of us who've been reading about the world of tomorrow but dreaming of the world of yesterday had better take another look at how things are stacking up and concede that these are the good old days.

Yes, sir. Take it from a traveler who from 1941 to 1945, as a civilian with privileges, sometimes got pretty close to war. . . . From now on, I want to stay at least that close to peace.

BOB HOPE

CONTENTS

CHAPTER		PAGE
1.	How About Another Peace?	1
2.	It's Best to Keep Moving	20
3.	Old Rocket Plane's Got Us	44
4.	Back to Abnormal, See?	60
5.	Don't You Know There's a Peace On?	86
6.	Worn World	105
7.	South Sea Island Makeshift	123
8.	From Bad to Würst	146
9.	Deutschland unter Allies	167
10.	To the Victors Belong the Spoiled	185
	P.S.	205
	P.P.S.	206
	N.B.	207
	Appendix No. One	207
	Appendix No. Two	207
	Epilogue	207
	Bibliography	207

CHAPTER 1

How About Another Peace?

WE'RE at peace. We're not enjoying it, but we're *at* it. And it's sensational what can happen in just one year *of* it.

We have famine in the midst of plenty and plenty in the midst of famine. The United Nations held meetings. But the meeting nations were never united. Great Britain's lion turned on Russia. The Russian Bear tried everything but Unguentine on Byrnes. And the whole UN setup got a cut out of Connecticut.

But we're doing all right. As soon as the war ended, we located the one spot on earth that hadn't been touched by war and blew it to hell.

Actually the most startling thing peace did for us was to send our Army and Navy back to fighting each other. During the war they proved that a unified command was essential to victory. So as soon as there was enough freedom from fear to plan a unified command, the Army and Navy each set out to prove it kept the other around just for laughs.

Don't get the idea I'm knocking laughs. Only there's a right way to get them and a wrong way to get them. And the way I get them, which is known as the Commando method ... strike hard and fast and get away in a hurry. People really won't believe that in June, 1946, we played thirty-three cities in twenty-nine days. Oliver Hardy, a veteran of many a vaudeville tour, said, "A trip like that must have been plenty hot."

It really wasn't. The way we traveled there was always a breeze. Covering the country in two Trans-Air Constellations we were always two or three jumps ahead of the FBI. And only a few weeks ahead of the CAA. It's wonderful traveling by air. And your laundry dries so much quicker.

We opened the tour in Spokane, Washington—which is Rand-McNally's name for Crosbyville—and played for eleven thousand paying customers and three thousand of Bing's relatives. He drove in from a near-by movie location to lead them. From Spokane we started accelerating. And to give you an idea how fast we traveled, we left Spokane with two rabbits—and when we got to Topeka, we had two rabbits.

That kind of thing doesn't really tire me, though. I'd have stayed on the road another month but I had to get back to Hollywood to start a picture with Dottie Lamour, *My Favorite Brunette*. I hope you'll like it. The opening scene shows President Truman waltzing with John L. Lewis. It's a fantasy. Remember those pictures that came out when they settled the coal strike? I mean where they were shaking hands? John L. with a lump of coal over each eye. And Truman with that Independence look ... "laughing on the outside, crying on the inside."

People said we were silly to make a trip that would take us through the Middle West and South in June. By the time

How About Another Peace?

we hit Oklahoma it hadn't rained in so long the trees were chasing the dogs. And when we got to Nebraska it was so dry they had to *pin* the stamps on the envelopes. So maybe we *were* silly. But so was the rest of the country. They came to see us.

So This Is Peace

But if the country was silly the way it spent money for entertainment, it was only being consistent with the political activities. Congress wanted to kill the OPA, so they passed a bill to extend it. And the President wanted it continued, so he vetoed the bill. Everybody suddenly became so interested in politics that the Republicans split into two groups, The Reactionaries and The Liberals; and the Democrats split into two groups, The Liberals and The Bilbos.

So nobody would be embarrassed by the fact that I didn't have a ticket, I sneaked in to the Jackson Day Dinner. And before we started discussing Truman's fancy necktie, I met one cabinet member and said to him, "I didn't know you were from Missouri."

He drew me aside and whispered, "Don't tell Harry, but I just happened to be going through on a bus."

Of course the President played the piano. This surprised me because it was after he'd signed the anti-Petrillo bill and Caesar still let him perform. It was the first time I'd heard Harry play and I must say he plays very well. Much better than *my* haberdasher. Us political forecasters are now confused. We don't know whether we should start Carmen Cavallero in the shirt business or get Cluett to quit Peabody and join José Iturbi. But I must confess, it was quite an impressive sight to see the President sitting there, playing "The Missouri Waltz," and then look out the window at Harold Stassen marching up and down outside, singing "It's Been a Long, Long Time."

But I'm really not interested in politics. It's just that my friendship with Crosby brought me in touch with the old Whig Party.

Actually, both parties are very worried. Everybody's so loaded with that government lettuce he can't spend that

How About Another Peace?

there's nothing the Republicans can promise. And all the Democrats have to do it explain why the Republicans won't sell it.

But with the people's pockets crammed with happy cabbage, the busiest key on the cash registers continues to be No Sale. And the consumer who expected a little courtesy when the war ended is getting what he expected . . . little courtesy.

Nineteen hundred and forty-six will go down in history as the year you looked for a haberdashery shop by hunting up a dark store with two clerks sitting behind empty counters playing gin rummy so they wouldn't hear the crowd of civilians in shorts pounding on the doors. And if you peeked into one of these men's clothing stores and saw three worried-looking gents trapped in their long underwear gazing at empty racks, the three men were probably Hart, Schaffner and Marx.

So This Is Peace

Bob Burns said the only way a friend of his, who's just been discharged from the Army, could get any clothes was to join the Navy. I asked one clothier, "What's become of men's clothes?" He gave me a straight answer. He said, "The women are wearing them."

For four long years of war, our advertisements and radio commercials were filled with promises. During the first year of peace, the promises were filled by advertisements and radio commercials. Almost the only way a woman could get a pair of nylon stockings was to appear on a quiz program. But I suppose nylons *will* be back by 1947, so I'll probably have to take a loss on that silkworm I've been feeding since 1942.

I really feel sorry for the gals, though. For years they looked at the ads for refrigerators and electric garbage-disposal units and sang, "Take Me to the Land of My Dreams." Finally they had to change to "When I Grow Too Old to Dream."

Peace didn't start essential oils flowing from the Pacific and the oil a girl could get from a Hollywood wolf wasn't worth packing. So we continued to save fat, which kept Sydney Greenstreet on the priority lists. And up to the very moment of going to press, C. B. de Mille still hadn't paid that dollar to the union. It's cost him more than that already, just *buying* his soap. And soap's very tough to get. I heard that Leopold Stokowski offered to play symphonic arrangements of "Rinso White" and "Wonderful Ivory Snow" if they'd give him enough of the stuff to start Gloria's mother in the laundry business. They wouldn't, so Gloria sent Mamma to the cleaner.

We were told that reconversion would be rapid and that before we knew it, postwar cars would be pouring off the assembly lines. After a year, they came off only in a trickle.

How About Another Peace?

And if you don't believe it, try crossing Hollywood Boulevard. It's some trickle!

Everybody wants to know where all the cars are coming from, including that sensational Los Angeles used-car impresario, Madman Muntz, who advertises, "I'll Give You a Million Dollars for Your Car, or Would You Rather Be a Pig?" and "You, Too, Can Sell Your Car to Madman Muntz and Be a Wealthy Pedestrian." *

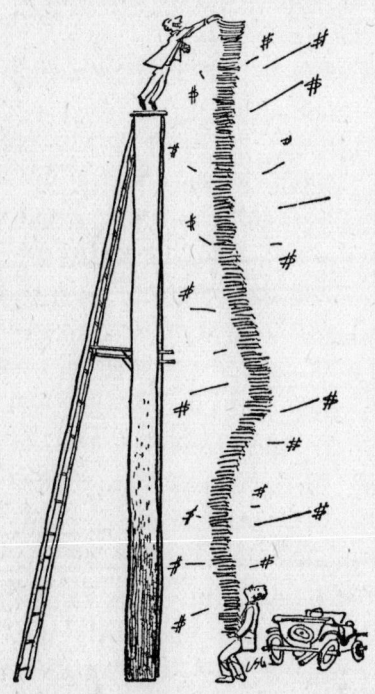

Besides the Madman, L. A. is loaded with other used-car caliphs; there's the Smiling Irishman, who smiles as he gives you "Top Dollar"; there's the Drooling Dane, who does business on the basis of the Golden Drool and has his advertising to prove it. And there's the Happy Hungarian, who feels so awful if you don't sell him your jalopy that he flings himself, moaning, into a caldron of hot goulash. I can remember when a used car was a cheap, secondhand automobile with an engine that ran. Peace turned it into an expensive, secondhand automobile with a dealer that runs.

The competition's so keen that all the money you need to

---

* As we go to press, Muntz does a radical about-face and plasters the town with a poster saying: MONEY ISN'T EVERYTHING (you fool). *GIVE* YOUR CAR TO MADMAN MUNTZ.

buy a 1927 wreck and wind up with four flat tires and a wallet to match is the OPA ceiling price; plus a reward to the guy who steered you to the lot; plus a bonus to the guy who runs the lot; plus your nearly new 1941 convertible. And they give you up to ninety minutes to pay. On this basis, the Smiling Irishman is outbidding the Pouting Pole. The Drooling Dane is making the Happy Hungarian look like the Stingy Scotchman. While the Eager Englishman is offering prices that make Madman Muntz look like Albert Einstein.

There's a story that a guy took a 1940 Buick he paid $1500 for and sold it to the Madman for $2000. He then took the two G's and paid $1200 for a 1938 Ford V-8, which he sold for $800 to buy a 1926 Cadillac runabout for $750, which he sold for $500. He took the five bills and invested them in a very snappy 1904 Lozier with acetylene brass lamps, demountable rims, folding windshield, one-man top, duster, and cap. And as he was driving this rig home, past the Warner Brothers studio, a prop man came running out and stopped him, saying, "We need that Lozier in a picture we're shooting!" and offered him $3000. Overjoyed at this smart business transaction, the guy took the three G's and went back to the lot where he'd sold his $1500 car for $2000 and bought it back for $3000. And, believe me, everyone says I got a bargain.

But what can you expect with new cars coming off the lines so slowly that it'll probably be well into 1947 before anyone except a Norwegian can honestly say fiord's out front?

But the 1947 jobs are really wonderful. One model actually makes is easier for you when you pass a blonde. The headlight squirts Sen-Sen and your right fender turns into an iron claw that grabs her and throws her into the back seat.

How About Another Peace?

This model has such a fancy horn that you not only need a driver's license, you also need a special union card signed by Petrillo, personally.

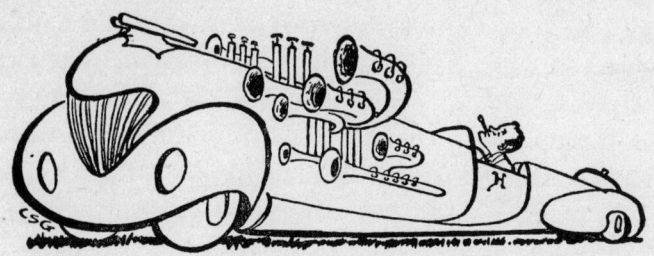

And those are only a few of the available gadgets. Cars assembled specially for California have sun-ray lamps instead of fog lights, so that when you hit a pedestrian he can get a tan on the way down. Another new gadget is the thing that makes it possible for you to park near a fire hydrant. You just back in wherever you want to and if there's a hydrant there, an automatic radar-operated arm shoots out and saws it off. Some civic officials feel this arrangement is all wet.

Not only have they installed push buttons for raising and lowering the windows and raising and lowering the top, one company even offers you a car with a button that raises and lowers the payment. It calls your friends and raises it, then sees the finance company about lowering it. This same outfit offers a special sports model where, if you're sitting in the back seat with your girl and she's not finding your dialogue very amusing, you just push a button and the Smiling Irishman pops out and laughs it up for you. Yes, sir, even the gadgets have gadgets.

And the center of gravity's so low I'm going to have to shorten the string on my yo-yo three inches. Of course they're only giving four tires with the new cars. So I'll keep my five old tires. The one around my waist and the four on my old car.

They're so tattered that every time I run over a pedestrian, my tires punish him for being careless by giving him fifteen lashes. Actually, I guess I'm the only driver in Hollywood who got over 5000 miles on his spokes. That's as good as anyone's ever done with a Cadillac. I have a Cadillac 16. Of course I didn't get it until '19.

It has four speeds: first, second, third, and kneel on the running board and push with the other foot. So, naturally, I wanted a new car. That kneeling wears out the pants. When I drove up to an automobile salesroom and asked to see a salesman, the man said, "We don't have salesmen any more. People are now so eager that if you want a car you go to the factory and wait there till they build one around you." Naturally, the car shortage has forced a lot of people to follow horses. And nowhere in the United States do they follow the horses and take them as seriously as they do in Hollywood. Busher's a bigger star than Lassie. Just for example, Hollywood's the only place in the world where horses run for Mayer (ouch!).

Still, in spite of this shortage of new cars, traffic in southern California reached such a state that they had to start running motion-picture shorts in all Los Angeles theaters begging people please not to get run over. And it's rumored that certain chain undertaking parlors immediately claimed this was in restraint of trade. The police say that if traffic gets any worse, east-west traffic will move in spring and fall, with north-south traffic moving in summer and winter. This will enable careful planners to spend their summers at the beach, their winters in the South, and their springs and falls in traffic jams.

How About Another Peace?

Traffic conditions in Los Angeles were considered impossible before the war, when some of the jalopies still had brakes, and if a car didn't look fit to be on the street, it was stopped by a policeman. But now, pedestrians are stopping cars. They're stopping so many of them that if you haven't a reservation in some emergency accident ward, you'd better not go out to mail a letter. It shows, though, what a great country the United States is. What other nation in the world would have an automobile-accident problem during an automobile shortage?

But the guy who really had a gripe about the car shortage was an ex-staff sergeant who came back to see me after our show in Dallas last June, where they made us play the Cotton Bowl so we couldn't pull the wool over anybody's eyes. His name was Steve Frazer and he told me he'd caught our show the year before when he was stationed at the Arles Staging Area right outside of Marseille.

"How'd you like the show?" I asked.

"I liked it *last* year," he said.

I said, "Thanks."

"You ought to thank me," he said. "I walked here."

"Why?" I asked.

"I thought maybe you could help me get a jeep. I'm a plumber and I need a jeep."

"What did you do during the war?" I asked.

"Drove a jeep," he said. "For a whole year I drove a jeep around Marseille till I didn't want to ride in a jeep again. I didn't even want to ride any more. I wanted to walk. I wanted to walk in Texas dust. Well, I got my wish. My post-war plan came true. I can't get a jeep and I'm walking in the Texas dust."

At the time Steve was at the Arles Staging Area when I saw

it in 1945, hundreds of thousands of guys were awaiting transshipment from the ETO to the Pacific, with all their equipment and vehicles. And in any one of the vehicle processing centers, as far as the eye could see, there were thousands upon thousands of jeeps, trucks, weapon carriers, recon and command cars. It looked like the back yard of my finance company.

Now you can buy that stuff as surplus property for a song. At least some people can. I bid one song for a bulldozer and they told me the best I could do for one of my songs was to get a gas mask. I wanted the bulldozer because there's nothing better for making a left-hand turn into Wilshire Boulevard.

Among the surplus offered for sale is an aircraft carrier. They're nice roomy boats. We've done shows on them. I'd have done more but every time I did a show on a flattop, somebody commented on the remarkable resemblance.

We used to work on the elevator that brings the planes from the hangar deck to the flight deck. It's a good idea. Every time you drop an egg, you go down with it.

An enterprising young GI might also pick up an old LST cheap and use it as a seagoing drive-in movie. You drive your car down to the beach, onto the ship, and go to sea while you sit in your car and watch a picture. It would be a wonderful thing for the movie industry. People couldn't be sure whether it was the weather or the picture that made them feel that way.

What a spot that Arles Staging Area was! There were thousands and thousands of men living in miles and miles of tents sitting around singing "Mairzy Doats and Dozey Doats but We Don't Want Those Tokyoats." The tents were pitched on a hot, dusty, windy, rocky, barren plain that

How About Another Peace?

really made a trip to Tokyo look like the Day's Best Bet. They had to truck in their water, and the bathroom facilities would have made even Chic Sale go over the hill.

So our little group started hamming it up for those guys, figuring that if they could stand living in a Marseille staging area, they could stand anything.

And just to give you an idea what I mean by that, Spike Jones and his City Slickers had been to Marseille ahead of us. As a matter of fact, Spike played France well before V-E Day. Spike and the City Slickers, Bing Crosby, Dinah Shore, and Fred Astaire were all in France at once right after D-Day. Each wanted to be the first into Paris. Spike almost made it. His boys and their cowbells were so close behind the Army that they got right to the gate of the city, when they were requested to go no farther. The request came from the people of Paris.

I asked Spike if, while he was in France, he played "Right in Der Führer's Face." He said he couldn't. Der Führer was going the other way.

But Spike really gets misty-eyed when he tells how his band played "La Marseillaise" for the French. He said it actually made the French people cry. Knowing Spike's music, you think you can understand why. But Spike's boys played the French national anthem straight. And the reason people cried was because it was the first time many of them had heard it in six years. There were little French boys and girls who had never heard that magnificent song of the French people.

Spike also told me that while they were there, Marseille had a tradition that when a really good visiting band came to town it played on the roof of the Hôtel Marseille. A band that wasn't so good played downstairs in the grill. Spike played for the underground. But they were the best people. We didn't get to play for them.

Our first show was in a big bowl set in the hills. It was called the General Ben (Yoo-Hoo) Lear Amphitheater and about 40,000 guys turned out in full force to yoo-hoo at our girls.

How About Another Peace?

At that time, our little unit 676 consisted of Jerry Colonna, The Stash; Gale Robbins, The Thrush; June Bruner, pianist and crooner; Ruth Denas, who also sang and pumped a squeeze box; Patty Thomas, who wore a small costume and danced; Roger Price, who did everything, including our laundry; and Jack Pepper, the ballast from Dallas who spent most of his time in some mess hall, making a big man of himself—a troupe of troupers never too tired to do another show and always willing, eager, and able to steal a scene or a laugh from guess who.

Between shows, I ran across a guy who had been a make-up man at Paramount, PFC Hal Lierile. Naturally, I rushed over to him, grabbed his hand, and said, "Hya, fella!"

He just looked at me blankly and said, politely, "Have we met somewhere before?"

He didn't recognize me with my street face on.

We hung around Marseille quite a while. There was no way out. And it was there I had my one and only encounter with the French press. It's not easy to give an interview through an interpreter who doesn't understand the language you're speaking. He kept urging me to speak English but I couldn't understand him because he kept urging me in French.

Firing questions at me were representatives from *Combat, La Marseillaise, Provençal, Rouge-Midi*, and the magazine *V*. Most of the correspondents were young men and women who had worked on underground papers during the occupation.

When I entered the room, one of them made a beautiful speech that lasted ten minutes and finished with the first question. The question was, "Who are you?"

This was kind of a tough one to answer, so I passed the buck to Colonna. He had it changed into francs and passed it to a man selling postcards. The correspondents then wanted to know who Colonna was. This was the toughest question of the day. Finally I told them he was a famous singer from L'Américan Opera.

Jerry then inhaled for two minutes and demonstrated his style of singing. The correspondents immediately went back underground.

The interview was arranged by the PRO, that's Public Relations Officer, in Marseille, Major Mark Finley. I'd known Finley as Publicity Director of the Don Lee Mutual Network in Hollywood. His public-relations job in Marseille was tougher. In 1944, the AAF had bombed German shipping in Marseille Harbor. Owing to bad wind, some of the bombs landed on the city and killed about 5000 Frenchmen. So they weren't too fond of Americans. In fact, I made Finley's work harder because they were just beginning to warm up to Americans again when I showed up. But Finley did a great job.

While in the Marseille area, I ran into a kid actor, Private Tommy Kelly, who had played the lead in the picture *The Adventures of Tom Sawyer* a few year ago. Tommy was twenty and he'd been in the 66th Infantry two years. I told him I'd seen him in *Tom Sawyer* and asked if he remembered me.

"No," he said, "I never saw *The Birth of a Nation*."

"Are you having any chance to practice your acting in the Army?" I asked.

"Not much," he said. "In the infantry the sergeants have all the lines. The only part an infantry PFC can get is a walk on ... and on ... and on!"

On our third day around Marseille it was so hot I kept

How About Another Peace?

Colonna on stage all the time. It was shadier for the girls, working under his mustache.

After the show we sweated out a chow line with a tough bunch of Joes who called themselves the Panther Division. And after grub we wandered over to where a baseball game was going on. There we made a big mistake. We got into the game.

The umpire, Warrant Officer Lewis Ficzer, was from my home town, Cleveland. He kept trying to give me the breaks, but the guys kept complaining that allowing me seven strikes made the innings too long. Of course Colonna played. As soon as they saw his stash they knew he was a bush leaguer. The gals, Gale, June, Patty, and Ruth, stood along the base lines and kept on the alert for every play that was made. In between they watched the game.

But it was rough. Those Panther Division Joes were short of regular baseballs, so they showed me how to be careful to hit the one they were using in a certain way so the pin wouldn't fall out.

So This Is Peace

After the game I went to the locker room (that's country-club slang for latrine) and spent a little extra time slicking down my hair because we were scheduled to give a show for about two thousand Army nurses and I wanted to give them a touch of Hollywood glamour. Then I found out that Victor Mature, the Bernarr Macfadden of Zanuck's Polo, Croquet, and Picture Factory, had been through about a week ahead of me and had filled out his chest for the gals. So when I arrived some of the babes were still circling, trying to come in for a landing.

But I won't say they didn't appreciate me. When I walked on stage and flashed my profile six of those nurses immediately formed a first-aid team and rushed onto the stage with splints. They were a wonderful bunch. I've said it once and I'll say it again, an Army nurse is a gal who holds a soldier's hand, stroke's his head, and expects his temperature to go down. Every one of the two thousand we played for was a combat nurse who'd had it in France and had volunteered for Pacific duty.

The only trouble with nurses is they're all officers and sometimes this causes trouble. One guy in Marseille strained his wrist trying to get his fingers in his mouth to whistle and salute at the same time.

Typical of those nurses was Virginia Sessoms of Asheville, North Carolina, old Professor Kay Kyser's home bailiwick. When I met Virginia, she'd been in the Army six years and wanted to get home as much as any other GI but she'd volunteered for duty in the CBI Theater. She had sixty-eight points and two battle stars, one received when her hospital in France was bombed and repeatedly strafed by Germans. She's five feet two, weighs a hundred and ten pounds, and can spot a goldbrick at fifty feet. I found that out when I complained about my aching back.

How About Another Peace?

The day we left Marseille we took special time off to say good-by to Warrant Officer V. W. Marston and his 589th Orchestra. His outfit filled in great between our eggs. It was a fine band, directed by Sergeant Dave Schulze, who used to blow a lot of trumpet for Harry James and Gene Krupa.

Another guy I looked up before we left was Lt. Bob Emil. What a job he had! He was Special Service Officer assigned to keep up nurse morale. When I went back to see him he said, "Bob, for the last time, I'm telling you, I positively do not need an assistant!"

That was only one of the things that made it tough saying good-by to guys who'd helped us out around Marseille, guys like PFC Julio Faraone of Providence. Julio was our driver. He'd been overseas for twenty-seven months and didn't know when he'd get home. But he said, "Believe me, Bob, when I do get back, Rhode Island's going to look awful big to me."

Of course one of our constant problems on all our trips was laundry. We never stayed in one spot long enough to get it done. But the guys in Marseille gave us a little twenty-four-hour service before we left and instead of a bill I found this poem, by PFC. T. Tooney, stuck in one of my shirts:

> *We are the laundry Commandos, it's true,*
> *We thrive on soap that's sour and blue,*
> *We work all day and half the night*
> *To keep your laundry nice and white;*
> *We sincerely hope when this is done*
> *You'll remember QM Laundry Number One.*
>   (Signed) 320th & 187th QM Laundry Depot.

Lots of guys fought that war doing jobs like that. They never got any glory and they never made any headlines. But without them the war would have taken a lot longer to win.

CHAPTER 2

It's Best to Keep Moving

From Alaska to Antibes, from Bizerte to Berlin, from Prestwick to Peleliu, from '41 to '45, wherever servicemen were sweating out the duration, I heard them trying to define peace in terms of what it meant to them. It was sort of a global "These Foolish Things Remind Me of You."

Then peace came and turned out to be more confusing than a Pepsodent broadcast originating from a cement mixer; which is different from "Cement Mixer" originating from a Pepsodent broadcast. Both could happen. But the latter is "Cement Mixer, Putti Putti," one of the more conservative compositions of the Slim Gaillard Trio's head man, Mrs. S. Gaillard himself.

Slim popularized his calculated insanity from a little cave called Billy Berg's on Hollywood's Vine Street, saying over the air, "Come down here:

We got Sandwiches, Melloreeney and Vout.
We got them ham an' egg sandwiches, them
   cheese sandwiches. We got meat sandwiches.
And the special for tonight is
Avocado and bourbon sandwiches . . .
On rye!"

It's Best to Keep Moving

Slim is a talented Negro musician and scat singer who speaks six languages, not including Mellorooney, Be-Bop, and Vout. He could have figured out that everybody's noggin-goo gets a little curdled after a war; copped a gander at the material that kept the pianolas pumping in 1918—stuff like "Ja-Da Ja-Da Ja-Da Jing-Jing-Jing," "K-K-K-Katy," "Doodle Doo Doo," "Oh, by Jingo" and "Ching-a-ling's Jazz Bazaar"—and figured we'd be putti putti for his cement mixer.

This, of course, brought on a rash of less inspired and original gibberish, including "One-zy, Two-zy, I Love You-zy," "Shoo-Fly Pie and Apple Pan Dowdy," "Frim Fram Sauce with the Ossapau and Chipaupa on the Side" and "Ashby dela Zooch Castle Abbey." There's nothing new about the the pattern. In 1918, after what Fibber McGee likes to tell Molly was "The *Big* War," the flappers took to wearing flat-heeled saddle oxfords, sweaters, and sloppy coats. So after

So This Is Peace

Old Global the hip chicks are wearing flat-heeled saddle oxfords, sweaters, and sloppy coats. That's progress.

And here's another sign of progress. It wasn't until after the war ended that my doctor had to give me a nerve tonic. Can you imagine giving me something for my nerve?

It's Best to Keep Moving

I had the prescription filled and put the bottle on the table. Dolores came down to breakfast, looked at the nerve tonic, then at me, and asked, "Which takes what?"

All I did was look at the nerve tonic and start to love all those people who used to say, "Well, after the war you'll get a nice change and rest." The old joke's still solid. The air lines are still getting my change and the hotels are getting the rest. But I shouldn't say that. Things really got easier. During the war we'd leave Hollywood every week to do our broadcast at some camp. Maybe we'd fly for six hours just to do a show in Denver. Imagine flying six hours from Hollywood to do a half-hour show in Denver. But things are different now. Much more easygoing! Now if we fly six hours from Hollywood we get to Cleveland.

Cleveland, that's the town I left to make a name for myself. I didn't like the names they were calling me there. But I really look back happily on those days that have gone by. Happily because they've gone by.

Nobody believes me when I tell them that back in those early days in Cleveland, John D. Rockefeller and I were business acquaintances. It's really true. I was in the newspaper business in those days. I sold them. And John D. used to patronize my stand on Euclid Avenue.

I can still remember one snowy winter evening when John D. handed me a ten-dollar bill. "I can't break this," I said, figuring he'd tell me to keep the change. He said, "*Get* the change!"

I said, "I'll trust you for the two cents."

J. D. said, "Son, always do business on a cash basis. I'll wait here while you run across the street for change.

So while I ran across the street and lost about five sales, John D. Rockefeller stood waiting in the snow. I always felt

So This Is Peace

he might have sold a few *Plain Dealers* instead of just standing there. But, then, maybe he didn't think I could afford to pay his salary.

I hadn't thought of J. D. except when buying a gallon of gas or changing a dime until the opening of the National War Fund Drive in Detroit in the winter of 1945. I was supposed to lay a few eggs as the cornerstones of the Detroit Drive and I was surprised to hear Edgar Guest, the poet, introduce me as one of the two men who had given the most money to the fund. The other was Rockefeller. I guess the loss of those five sales didn't hurt too much. The War Fund's income from *I Never Left Home* put me on J. D.'s team.*

But to get back to Cleveland, that's what we did on March 19, 1946; we being Frances L., Skinnay E., Jerry C., and the guy who peddles P. with I.

As our big Constellation flew in over Cleveland Airport, I looked down and a big lump rose up in my throat. It was the apple I'd swallowed over Albuquerque. The trip took eleven hours and forty minutes from Los Angeles to the Carter Hotel in Cleveland. That's seven hours from L. A. to Cleveland Airport and four hours and forty minutes to the Carter Hotel. I can't walk very fast carrying two suitcases. But I didn't mind. I remembered the day I left home and how my father predicted that I'd go a long way as he nailed up the door of the boxcar to make sure.

The crowd at the airport frightened me. They were screaming and hollering. Naturally, the ropes were up. But I demanded a fair trial. And I still love the old town.

A good portion of my family still lives there, so I have quite a bit of money invested in Cleveland. Some of my folks

---

* PUBLISHER'S NOTE: The income from *So This Is Peace* goes to "The Hope Fund" to care for several branches of the Hope family.

It's Best to Keep Moving

were glad to see me. Others said they were just as happy getting it through the mail. But I have one brother who's doing fine in Canton, Ohio. Another's doing *five* at Columbus.

After I cleaned up at the Carter Hotel (the janitor's not a very good gin-rummy player) they drove me through the streets. But I finally managed to elude them. And in spite of all this, the old town seemed warmer and friendlier than it ever had before. Even the wind off the lake didn't seem as cold as it once was. Of course on this trip I was wearing underwear.

My arrival had been arranged to coincide with Cleveland's Sesquicentennial Celebration. And there were signs everywhere saying, "A hundred and fifty years old!" I'm still trying to find the guy who put them all under my pictures. I told Skinnay Ennis I'd show him the street I was born on. He said, "What was the matter, couldn't you afford a hospital?" So I explained that Cleveland had very long traffic signals.

Of course I tried to visit the house I was born in. It was a humble little three-room cabin ... kitchen, bedroom, and a long walk. And when I walked through my old neighborhood another lump was in my throat. It was the only safe place to carry my wallet.

Naturally, I went back and paid a visit to my old school. I saw the same old room. And I didn't see the same old teacher and her ugly face because it cost Ed Gardner a lot of dough for mentioning his old teacher on a Duffy's Tavern broadcast.

But I did go to my old third-grade room. I sat at the same desk. And there was the same old inkwell ... the same old primer ... and the same old shaving kit. They're very proud

So This Is Peace

of me at that school, though. Yes, sir, and over my old desk at Fairmont High, it says, "Bob Hope slept here."

I spent a whole afternoon just wandering around Cleveland, looking up old landmarks. And I was surprised to find how many of them were married. But the biggest thrill of my trip to Cleveland was renewing my friendship with a former golf partner and one of the outstanding political figures of the state of Ohio: the Governor, His Excellency Frank J. Lausche. That's how I introduced the Governor on our broadcast from Cleveland. And here, with some notes, is part of the script that the Governor played as well as any guest we've ever had:

(Applause)

Gov: Thanks, Bob. And thank you, Democrats!

Hope: Welcome to the Pepsodent Show, Governor. (*He was getting his from the Democrats and I was getting mine from Pepsodent.*)

Gov: Bob, I can only say it's a pleasure to appear with one of America's outstanding personalities.

Hope: NO WONDER THIS GUY'S GOVERNOR! I even saw a Republican applauding.

Gov: You saw a Republican applauding? (*The Governor reads a nice straight line.*)

Hope: Well, he wasn't exactly applauding. He was clicking two Bricker buttons together. But, Governor, it was really nice of you to consent to appear on my program.

Gov: Oh, that's all right, Bob. I don't run for re-election until this fall and by then the voters may forget.

Hope: Which reminds me, Governor, don't you think you could find me some sort of a political job? You know, radio's pretty shaky. You never know when the sponsor's going to put the cap on the tube. I'd just like a little something in the day coach of the official gravy train . . . sort of a small pig's knuckle in the pork barrel. How about me going to banquets with you and sneering at Republicans?

Gov: Bob, please—you have the wrong idea. In Ohio we always play ball with the Republicans. Of course we make

So This Is Peace

sure they don't spend too much time *at bat!* But you don't live in Cleveland any more, do you, Bob?

Hope: Nope.

Gov: And you make pretty good money now, don't you?

Hope: Well, not bad. What about it?

Gov: Bob, I have a lot of influence. But after this year, I'll just have to stop your relief check. (*This forced me to change my vote.*)

Hope: Well, summer's coming. I can always reopen my Frozen Custard booth out at Euclid Beach. Oh, say, Governor —tell me confidentially, is that rumor true that you have ambitions to get to the White House?

Gov: Why, Bob, how did a rumor like that ever start?

Hope: Last week a piano teacher was seen sneaking in your back door.

Gov: I guess you've been pretty busy since you've been back in Cleveland, eh, Bob?

Hope: Yes, I haven't even had time to go back and see my old home.

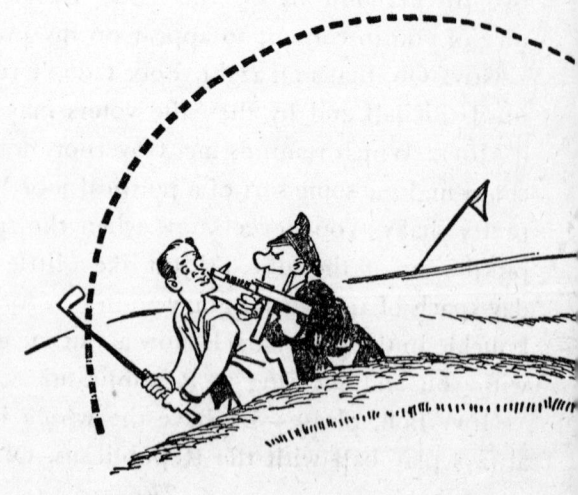

It's Best to Keep Moving

Gov: Oh, I'm sorry about that, Bob. But I guess I forgot to tell you about our recent slum-clearance program. But I want you to be my guest at the National Golf Open at Canterbury.

Hope: Oh, no, you don't, Gov. You can't rope me into another golf game after that last one.

Gov: You're just jealous because I won.

Hope: Well, no wonder. Who can beat a governor?

Gov: What do you mean?

Hope: When I made a hole in one, the Police Commissioner rushed over, shoved a machine gun in my face, and said, "That was a wonderful shot the Governor just made. Now let's see what *you* can do."

Gov: Anyway, Bob, I want to thank you sincerely for bringing your show back to Cleveland. And I want to add another word of thanks for the many, many things you've done to improve the city of Cleveland.

Hope: What improvement did I make? I left Cleveland in 1928.

Gov: Well, that doesn't leave me much to say . . . you *asked* the question and answered it, too. (*There was wild applause after this, naturally.*)

That was the end of our broadcast with the Governor. And that's why I have to keep moving. Even if I didn't want to it isn't easy to stop what you've been doing for five years. A way of living, like any other habit, is something you can't just quit. You have to taper off. A lot of GI's thought they could drop back into civilian life without ever missing reveille. But a lot of living and a lot of memories are mixed up with bugle calls, mess kits, and B-bags.

I was driving to the studio one day early in 1946 and picked up a guy who was thumbing a ride. That's something he probably wouldn't have been doing if it hadn't been for his Army training. He had a discharge button in his lapel, his clothes were prewar, and he told me he'd seen my show in the ETO. But he rode with me, anyway. Those guys are great. Not one of them carried a grudge.

I asked him how he liked being a civilian again. He just shook his head and smiled. I asked him if he had a job. He just shook his head and smiled. He didn't seem to have any real enthusiasm for the life he'd looked forward to and longed to get back to for twenty-six months. Then we passed a corner where a guy in an Army uniform was standing. He had the Timberwolf patch on his shoulder. All of a sudden my rider came to life and he almost shouted, "Stop the car; I want to get out and talk to that soldier."

"Know him?" I asked.

"Well, not exactly, but sort of."

"What do you mean?"

"He's from my old outfit. Let me out." I stopped the car. The guy said, "Thanks," and went back to talk to a friend he'd never met.

We civilians are the same way. None of us is really able to get back to normal the way we thought we could. And that's really why I thought I had to keep traveling.

Not to travel just didn't seem normal. Pretty soon there were only a few service camps left to do. This would have made me very disconsolate if I hadn't made a record album [*] of some of my shows at service camps. Nowadays it is very encouraging after broadcasting for the civilians to hurry home, put on the record of one of my Army shows, and glow happily in the knowledge that I was the greatest comedian who ever played the Yuma Army Air Base.

Of course, there are still plenty of hospitals to play. Funny, you never know what your audience is going to be or whom you're talking to. For instance, at Dibble General Hospital in San Francisco, we were doing an intimate little show for a small group of badly handicapped veterans, when an ambulatory case wandered into the room, leaned against the wall, took a great big sandwich out of a paper bag, and began to eat it . . . the sandwich, of course.

Naturally, this took the men's attention away from me. They all turned around to stare at the character eating the sandwich. So I said, "Well, what are you going to do, stand there and eat all by yourself?"

He understood what I meant, walked across the small room

---

[*] PUBLISHER'S NOTE: It's another racket. Hope's Capitol Record album of service shows now available at all music stores and the front gate of the Hope home.

to the little platform I was standing on, and offered me a bite. I took it, said thanks and "How you feeling?"

He said, "How *you* feeling?"

I said, "Fine!"

He said, "Fine!"

There was a short pause and I said, "Well, that's the end of that conversation."

Without any hesitation whatsoever he said, "It should be!"

Just then two men came up to my sandwich-eater and one said, "We missed you in the other room."

The guy said, "I know. I left there."

"Where'd you go?"

"In here."

"Let's get out of here."

I said, "Wait a minute, don't go away. This guy just topped me."

"That figured," one of the two men said. "But nevertheless, we have to take him back to the mental ward."

What disturbed me was that we had a well-balanced conversation.

Anyway, that shows why you really can't do hospital shows that'll give the patients much fun and broadcast them.

Life to a guy in a hospital takes on an entirely different meaning. His perspective is different, his viewpoint, his whole bed-panorama.

Naturally, we duck out to Birmingham General Hospital once in a while. Birmingham is very near Hollywood. In fact, I've heard soldiers say that the word Birmingham is San Fernando Valley for . . . "thermometer, wonderful treatment, great equipment, and 'get back in bed, we'll tell you when you're well enough to chase the nurses.' "

I'll never forget the first time I went out there. I phoned and told them I'd like to come, and the nurse said, "Of

It's Best to Keep Moving

course we'd be glad to have you, Mr. Hope. But we don't think we can help you much."

I asked to talk to either Sergeant Desi Arnaz or Sergeant Cully Richards. Richards answered, and I said, "Do you think the patients will pan me?"

Cully said, "Careful, Bob, that's a delicate word in a hospital."

But when I finally arrived they gave me a typical military hospital reception ... a twenty-one-atomizer salute.

You'd be amazed how those guys who are recuperating speed around the corridors in wheel chairs. I guess those chairs seem slow after P-38's, so the men are pretty reckless. I asked one guy how much longer he had to stay at Birmingham and he said, "I've been cured for a month. All I have to do now is serve out the last ninety days of my traffic sentence."

Which brings up the novel way they have of telling how a man is doing. They push a magazine rack through the wards and when a guy asks for *Esquire* he's passed the crisis.

We make it kind of a point to celebrate Christmas at Birmingham at least once a year. We generally try to make it around the 25th of December.

Naturally, they have a typical Army Christmas tree, a star on top, two oak leaves halfway down, and three privates painting the bottom.

The whole Christmas is done in true Army fashion. Santa Claus can't come down the chimney till he's been briefed on the roof. I played Santa once. I thought I had a good disguise. I wore whiskers and stuffed a pillow under my belt, but the feathers started to come out and one guy said, "Look, Joe, he's been laying 'em so long he's starting to molt."

The main event, of course, is Christmas dinner. When

everything is all set, a major stands up and says, "Okay, men, synchronize your watches."

Then in comes the turkey, the major shouts, "This is it!" and the battle of the bulge is on.

Naturally, the turkey is brought in on a stretcher with a thermometer in its . . . mouth. And before a lieutenant starts to carve, it's prepared for surgery. He then puts on rubber gloves and every five seconds yells for oxygen.

Those guys, though . . . they may be in the hospital but they don't eat sick. How they go after that food! Before I started to eat I said, "How's the stuffing?" A guy stuck his head out of the turkey and said, "Fine!" The soldier across from me swallowed a leg and second joint whole. I said, "What about the bones?"

He said, "Fine. Hand 'em over!"

But the big advantage of eating with soldiers in a *hospital* is that you can get bandaged afterwards.

After dinner, this was in late 1944, one of the doctors showed me an Army invention that the medical men had worked out for civilian practice. It was a stethoscope that counts your money while they're listening to your chest.

But, as I started to point out, with a different kind of show necessary at hospitals, we found that in order to keep our broadcast traveling we'd have to try playing college campuses. They weren't bad. After all, a big college campus is just Camp Pendleton with professors. And, under the GI Bill of Rights, we sometimes even met some of the same guys.

One of the major provisions of the GI Bill of Rights concerns the veteran's education. The government wanted to make sure that after a year or two of fighting and fraternizing the boys hadn't missed out on their education. This has resulted in an occasional impasse. Stanford was the first to report a war-born *faux pas* when a handsome sergeant turned in two chocolate bars to a young blonde physicist instead of the expected "Treatise on Vapor Density." An enterprising Seabee caused chaos in a quiet Minnesota classroom by appearing in a Nylon-stocking cap pulled down over his ears. And it's becoming increasingly difficult to interest young men in the fact that Hannibal crossed the Alps on an elephant when any fool can plainly see it takes a Missouri mule to get you anywheres these days. Reports from various campuses are that it has been exceedingly difficult on the boys who have taken their biology firsthand and arrived inside the ivy walls with a wife and a baby. They seem to be mixing up their chemistry and baby formulas. In fact, they flunked one boy at Michigan for insisting that water was made from two parts hydrogen and one part Pablum. But the colleges are trying, and I expect a deep bow is due the president of Princeton who, on learning a boy had got his diploma and become a father the same day, presented the lad with a three-cornered sheepskin.

It was really wonderful playing colleges. You could always blame the rotten eggs on the chem. lab. One of the first campuses we played was the University of Southern California. And what a wonderful reception I got! The president drove me to the broadcast. After the show I walked home with an unemployed coal passer from the boiler room.

At Stanford I had lunch with the faculty. They were very nice. They said my appearance at Stanford would be of great benefit to the students. But I still can't understand why they put the psychology students in the front row.

Naturally, whatever college we played, I tried to dress collegiate, although when we were at the University of Arizona it got a little warm wearing raccoon shorts.

So This Is Peace

One of the most interesting things about going from college to college was trying to find a professor who hadn't written a book. And the professors said one of the interesting things about meeting me was trying to find out *how* I wrote one.

I had some other interesting experiences, too. At the University of California at Berkeley, I happened to be wearing my hair long. We were shooting the picture *Monsieur Beaucaire* at the time. I walked across the campus and got elected the New Campus Queen.

And, speaking of shooting the picture *Monsieur Beaucaire,* the critics all said they should have shot the star. At Berkeley

It's Best to Keep Moving

I met a very pretty coed who told me her father was in grapes. It turned out the grapes were in her father. Coed, that's a pair of horn-rimmed glasses and a pair of bobby sox separated by a sloppy-Joe sweater.

But I shouldn't make fun of coeds. I can remember my college days. They made me sit between two pretty coeds and flunked me for not paying attention. I was a track star in college. I sold racing forms.

When I was going to college, my father used to drop into see me on *his* way to class. I even had one of those short college-boy haircuts. Mine was so short they had to cut it from the inside. They called me Velour Head Hope. My hair stood up so, it looked as if I was always listening to Orson Welles.

While at college, I went around for six years with a beautiful blonde coed and then something separated us. She became a sophomore. She said she could only love an athlete. Well, I played football when I was a kid. I had the toughest team on our block ... until a family with boys moved in. But anyway, I went out for football and finally made the scrub team. I was in charge of the soap. But I really learned the game. It got so I knew every trick of the trade. You learn a lot sitting on the bench with the coach.

Finally we played such a tough opponent everybody got into the game. Those guys against us played so rough that where they came from the worst penalty you could get was one yard. And that was for pulling a knife on the referee's mother. I went into the line, and the tackle opposite me weighed over three hundred pounds. I was afraid to face him on the first play. After that it was different. So was my face.

It's Best to Keep Moving

When he saw me he turned around to his team and yelled, "Hey, fellas, lookit the fancy pants I got. His ears got holes in 'em!"

But I was light and fast, in those days, and during the first half I was all over the field. It took the doctors that long to gather me up.

But when I got to Hollywood and began working I put on some weight and became a member of the All-Paramount Football Team. Jack Oakie was quarterback, remember? I played right half. Crosby was left half and W. C. Fields was full.

But enough of my youthful experiences. To get back to the colleges we played early in 1946, we really hit some very unusual campuses. Take the University of Nevada, for instance. It's in Reno. And between the gambling tables and the divorce courts, the most popular courses are, naturally, higher mathematics. Math courses are full of freshmen trying to figure out how many times three plus four goes into a bankroll. I'm told that even in the grade schools, the children in Reno start arithmetic by learning that when you substract one from one you get a divorce.

So for a while, instead of playing service camps, we traveled from one college to another, rubbing shoulders with professors and hoping a little education would rub off. It finally did and we got wise enough not to try to be smarter than the college kids. Especially in Nevada. Nevada, that's Monte Carlo with cowboys.

And how well I remember the last time I saw Monte Carlo. It was in the summer of 1945. We were on the French Riviera, doing shows for the officers and men in United States Army Rest Areas. A new kind of thing was going on in that territory where the high-society guys and gals used to tilt a teacup. The place was so full of Yanks that after sundown the whole coast tilted.

The occupation troops resting around Nice were all combat forces. And every man in the area had found the going very rugged. So it was great for them to relax in the setting the Army fixed up, and it was some setup!

Instead of armbands, the MP's wore halos and smiled at privates without ties. Anyone who said "sir" automatically got his mouth washed out with borax. Saluting was prohibited. And every Thursday they brought in a truckload of chicken colonels and stood them on the corners so the enlisted men could walk by and sneer.

The men lived in the luxury hotels that had cost European royalty twenty or thirty king-sized clams a day. They could have anthing they wanted in the way of boats, cars, bicycles, or sports equipment. At night there were plenty of sports, too, and night clubs with good music. Food was plentiful and wonderful, and beautiful Red Cross girls came around after lunch to burp the EM.

If a soldier happened to get hold of some bonded ice that that was a little too strong for him and lost part of his week end, the MP's never raised an eyebrow. They just looked in his pocket, found out where he belonged, and tucked him into bed.

Between shows at Nice, before we had time to go to Monte Carlo, we ducked over to Grasse to gander the perfume industry. It was already going strong! And I do mean strong. Of course, it hadn't gotten back to its full prewar stench. Nevertheless, my nose was eligible for the Purple Heart.

I wouldn't want to go on record as saying the perfumes they were then producing at Grasse smelled romantic, but one day an east wind blew some of the scents from Grasse to

It's Best to Keep Moving

Nice and eight sergeants proposed marriage . . . to each other.

"When do we go to Monte Carlo?" Colonna asked after we'd been to Grasse.

"Our next stop," I said, "is Cannes."

"Watch your language, Hope! There are gentlemen present," Colonna barked.

Cannes was the Riviera Recreational Center for officers. They got almost as courteous treatment as the enlisted men got at Nice. At Cannes, for example, it was a rule that all second lieutenants must be called *Mister* Shavetail. The bellboys were full colonels and General Omar Bradley was the house detective.

So This Is Peace

Instead of oak leaves, the majors all wore hibiscus blossoms.

The weather along the Riviera is a combination that would delight the amalgamated Chambers of Commerce of Los Angeles and Miami. I asked what made it so warm and pleasant. And I was told that across the bay at Juan-les-Pins there was a rest area for Army nurses and WAC's. One lieutenant made a fortune renting out his binoculars at a dollar a minute. But I wired home for more money.

We also got a bang out of driving around the Riviera, seeing the elaborate German defenses, the concrete gun emplacements and the huge, camouflaged pillboxes that were never used because we outflanked the Krauts and caught them with their pillboxes down.

On the Riviera we ran into Sonja Henie and Grace Moore. Sonja's a good skate and Grace is sort of a Dinah Shore with an extra lung.

We took a four-hour flight down the coast to do a show for 10,000 restees in a motorcycle-racing bowl, but someone should have explained to the management that ours was a different type of entertainment. Every time I went on stage, three French mechanics rushed out and tried to change my spark plugs. I wouldn't have minded if they'd been successful.

But it was after this show that we finally got to visit Monte Carlo.

About ten in the morning we took off in a motorboat and cruised along the French coast until we came to the U.S.S. *Gridley,* a destroyer playing hooky from Admiral Halsey's Third Fleet. Naturally, we waved and they invited us on board for lunch. So we put on an impromptu show for them on the afterdeck, after which Gale Robbins and Tor-

It's Best to Keep Moving

pedoman 2/c R. C. Clelland, of Philadelphia, did a jitterbug routine that almost sank the ship.

We then cruised on to Monte Carlo, sometimes known as the Mediterranean version of Las Vegas. The town was off limits to all military personnel. Because they didn't want some soldier, sailor, or marine to walk in there and clean out the joint.

We had no trouble finding the Casino. It's a big domed building with a large IOU flag flying at half mast. Right next door is the haberdashery where they sell all the shirts their customers lose. To save trouble we left ours as we went in.

CHAPTER 3

Old Rocket Plane's Got Us

IF YOU think that was a fast trip we made from the University to Nevada to Nice and Monte Carlo, wait till you really get a load of jet propulsion. That's life catching up with a radio sound effect. When we do a sketch on the air we say, "Let's go to Skinnay Ennis' house" ... the sound man makes a certain noise ... and we're there! That's jet propulsion ... a sound effect you can ride in.

And they're developing it so fast, in conjunction with atomic energy, that pretty soon a kid in Chungking will holler, "Hey, Ma, I'm goin' to London to play softball with some Detroit kids" ... climb onto his jet-propelled scooter and woosh off so fast he won't hear his mother yell, "Be home for dinner by six; your father has to get an early start to a poker game in Buenos Aires."

Yes, sir. That jet propulsion is really something. It's the answer to all of us who've wondered what it would be like to hang onto the stick of a skyrocket. Of course the English really had their dose of jet propulsion during the buzz-bomb period. It got pretty rough. They'd hear the whine of one of those V-1's coming over and everyone would stop to listen. If the noise cut out, you had about ten seconds to crawl down a gopher hole and pull the hole in after you.

David Niven, Samuel Goldwyn's threat to Ronald Colman, who fought with the British Army for the entire length of the war and rose from subaltern to father, gets pretty grim when he talks about England during the era of the buzz bombs. David says he took Garson Kanin, the young Hollywood director and author of the successful Broadway play, *Born Yesterday*, to see a ballet during the buzz-bomb period.

By way of trying to warn Kanin that the people of London were a little unnerved by the frightening things against which there was virtually no defense, David said in that way the English have, "If people seem to act a bit strange and jumpy from time to time, old boy, think nothing of it. They've had a little trouble here, you know."

As he was saying this, the buzzing became audible . . . the buzzing that warned of sudden death in flight. Everyone froze. The dancers seemed to retard into slow motion and began ad libbing into groupings for mutual protection. No one said a word. There was nothing to say. Suddenly, the way a thunderstorm breaks, silence galvanized everyone's blood as the bomb cut out. There were just ten seconds. Just time for a short prayer.

Kanin looked at Niven. Niven looked at the floor. The air was so silent you could hear a heartbeat. Then a terrific, shattering explosion near by, and Kanin shouted involuntarily, "Holy God!"

A little old lady leaned over, tapped him on the shoulder, put her index finger to her lips, and said, "Sssh!" as she pointed to where the music had started and the dancers had resumed their routine.

But now, jet propulsion is being used for man's good, it says here. And when it gets as common as incandescent light, I wonder if we'll all dress like Flash Gordon . . . and what's more important, will the girls all dress like Dale.

Of course, I know all about jet propulsion because our house in North Hollywood isn't far from Lockheed. We moved there during the war so it would be easy for Dolores and the kids to get to work. And the other day one of the newest Lockheed jet jobs did a quick turn over our property. Tony came running into the house, screaming, "Daddy, a noise just flew by."

Poor Buck Rogers. Can't you see him sitting home behind his Dewey button, dreaming of the "good old days," when his transportation was considered something flashy and extreme?

So with the world generating the kind of speed we're building up to, how can a guy find the peace he promised himself? How can you relax with an atom bomb under your pillow and the knowledge that every time you lean over to pick a four-leaf clover the world goes whizzing by your window? Well, when you lean over, it may not go whizzing by your window; but just the same, you'd better look out. Any minute someone could let go with an experimental nuclear chain reaction and the world would be whizzing by the moon.

There isn't an awful lot of peace left in the world when man finds he can travel faster than sound. If we can maintain the present rate of acceleration, we're really in for something. Frankie can broadcast a chorus in New York and, if he plays his cards right, take a bow in Chicago, and sign autographs in Los Angeles before the applause dies down. It won't be long before a salesman in Cleveland can quote a wrong price to a prospect in Kansas City, hop a plane, get to the customer's office, and tell him to hang up before he hears that same wrong price.

I'm planning to incorporate an air-freight and -express line that will use only atom-powered planes. Naturally, it will be called the Atom's Express Company.

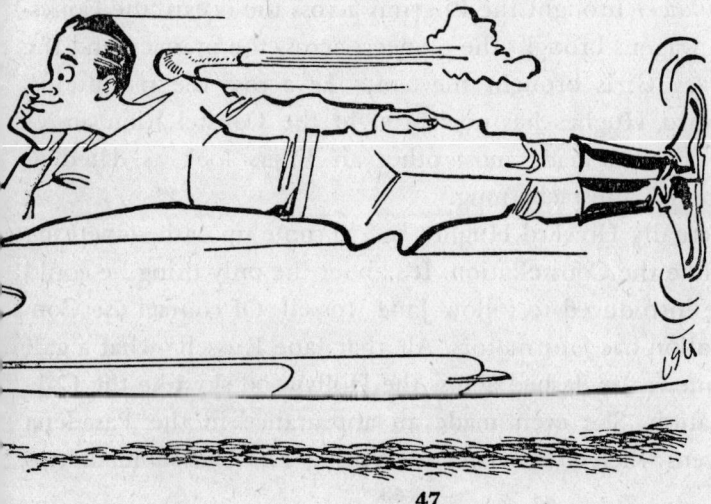

So This Is Peace

It's really foolish to make jokes about what's going on. This day and age is catching up with the silliest sally. All us steady readers of that classic old gag book, *A Slow Train Through Arkansas,* know the one about the man who stuck his head out of the train window in Little Rock to kiss his wife good-by and kissed Bob Burns in Van Buren. What's impossible about that with jet propulsion? Only with j.p. you stick your head out the window and it flies off. No one could survive that speed, except, of course, Crosby. With his flaps he'd land in a long slow glide.

Over seven hundred people actually volunteered to be aboard the Navy ships to be used as targets off Bikini. This is the beginning of a natural cycle to start the development of people with enough stamina to take what science dishes out. And it won't take long to develop this kind of superman. Just look at the bobby-soxers, the mothers of the future, who are already strong enough to get into a Sinatra broadcast. And the pioneer women thought *they* were rugged.

Believe me, the world has come a long way since the *Mayflower* brought the Pilgrims across the ocean, the Conestoga wagons brought the pioneers across the prairies, and the Harvey Girls brought the Santa Fe across the mountains. Howard Hughes has now brought the Constellation across the sky and made most other air liners look as dated as Colonna's mustache mug.

Actually Howard Hughes *had* to come up with something big like the Constellation. It's about the only thing he could have introduced to follow Jane Russell. Of course, the Constellation has *four* motors. Ah, that Jane Russell—what a gal!

Jane really flashed across the Hollywood sky like the Constellation. She even made an appearance in the Pasadena heavens when a sky writer advertising *The Outlaw* made two large circles under her name . . . and dotted them. Jimmy Durante got the gal's name barred from the networks by teaming her handle with a timpani solo so that every time he said Jane Russell the timpanist took two socks at his kettle between the Jane and the Russell. It created an effect almost as startling as Jane's decolletage. But back to aviation.

To inaugurate the nonstop coast-to-coast daily run of the Constellation, Howard Hughes flew a load of big movie names to New York for the week end. In the party were Cary Grant, Paulette Goddard, William Powell, Veronica Lake, Jack Carson, and Frank Morgan. Morgan also took quite a load east. Walter Pidgeon was also included in the party in case someone wanted to send back a message.

My first trip on the Constellation was that flight home to Cleveland. It was a wonderful ride. Beside the pilot and copilot, the ship carries an engineer. And beside the engineer you'll find two stewardesses. And beside the two stewardesses you'll find me. But it's really not the two stewardesses or the four motors or the high speed that I like about the Constellation. It's that engineer. He's my type. All he does is sit and gaze at instruments, leaving the two pilots to devote all their time to flying and answering passengers' questions. Answering questions is tough because by the time a passenger has managed to say "Where are we?" and the pilot looks to see, you're somewhere else.

But the engineer hasn't a hard job like that. He just sits and gazes at about 17,000,000 dials. There's one dial I could read. It said 6:15. Thought I couldn't tell time, eh? But the flight engineer knows what they *all* mean. They make it possible for him to anticipate trouble and prevent it. That gives me a comfortable feeling. When a guy's flown over 300,000 miles, he begins to wonder how much longer he can keep

So This Is Peace

up. So I'd like to fly all the rest of my miles with a guy whose eye is on the dials. I don't want any more of that "everyone put on your parachutes" routine we had in Alaska. Or even that little crash landing that brought our merry party to the shores of Australia.

We were on our way home after a swing around the Pacific and had just done some shows at Noemfoor, in New Guinea. While we were doing the show, they shot a Jap about twelve hundred yards from our stage. Some people say the Jap was just the victim of bad shooting. But when they told me how close the Japs were, I put in a call for my agent.

No kidding, I thought I'd seen the most rugged kind of warfare in North Africa and Sicily until I got a gander at what those guys in the Pacific were up against. Just keeping alive on most of those jungle islands was a man-sized struggle against almost man-sized bugs. And I don't mean Japs.

It took colossal courage for the kids from the U. S. A. to lie in the dark of a crawling jungle and face eternity. They took plenty of punishment, mental as well as physical, to keep us safe. But, as one guy at Noemfoor said, "We know that as long as Hope and his gang are in the Pacific, the folks at home are safe."

At Biak we played for the 31st Division—an outfit that had fought the most campaigns in the Pacific. They'd seen more action than Tommy Manville's best man. The day we put on a show for them there was a half-mile perimeter. And the men were fully armed and ready to fight at any time. We didn't find this out till later. But it didn't help the gags much to have B-24's taking off every few minutes to bomb a peninsula half a mile away. I want to tell you it's not easy to stand up there and peddle your jokes while looking down a carbine. It's like playing a benefit for the Purple Gang.

This, as I said—or did I?—was en route to Australia in a big PBY. We'd got safely away from our last show . . . and I was standing behind our pilot, Lieutenant Frank Ferguson, watching him fly the big boat. Suddenly one motor conked out and the plane began to lose altitude. *I* began to lose other things. We threw everything we owned overboard to lighten the load. Colonna was almost forced to shave. We'd flown thousands of miles over water in land planes. Now we were in a Catalina Flying Boat and in trouble, and where would we be—over land!

Fergie looked back and said, "I thought I told you to throw everything overboard to lighten the load."

"We did," I said. "All the cigarettes, the ship's tools, and the baggage."

So This Is Peace

"What about those cases of Scotch?" he hollered.

"I'm saving those for a sick friend," I told him.

"Who's the sick friend?" Colonna asked.

"Me."

But I kept smiling all through it . . . a great big, foolish, frozen grin with my teeth chattering like a typewriter. It wasn't that I was scared. It was cold up there.

Fergie finally found a strip of water and landed us on a sand bar. It was the first bar I ever fell *into*.

There was a big silence after we landed while the ice water in our veins turned back to blood. Finally Colonna climbed out into a full four inches of water and screamed for help. A local fisherman pulled him out and before he asked who we were or where we came from, he asked, "Have you any American cigarettes?"

I said I'd be glad to trade him two packs of Old Golds for a pint of Type O. I guess I looked pretty pale because the fisherman just said, "Thank you, Mr. Sinatra."

Captain Lanny Ross of the Army, and Lt. Comdr. George Halas, owner-coach of the Chicago Bears, steered us around Sydney, where we played all the Army and Navy hospitals.

The people down there were wonderful. So was their hot water. They kept asking me when we were going to make *The Road to Australia*. It's still not a bad idea, either. Crosby's finished with *Road* pictures. But I could replace him with a kangaroo. Who'd know the difference? They both have pouches. And with a setup like that I might win Dorothy Lamour.

We hated to leave Australia, but we made the 8000-mile hop home in fifty hours. When Dolores met us at Burbank, I said proudly, "Well, here we are. A hundred and fifty shows! Thirty thousand miles. And made the last hop of eight thousand miles in fifty hours."

Old Rocket Plane's Got Us

"What kept you?" Dolores asked. She must have had an advance tip on the speeds that were coming.

But as the plane was coming in for a landing, Tony, who'd come to the airport to see us arrive, kept waving and calling "Good-by, Daddy."

When we got home we all sat around and I got out my souvenirs and bored the whole family with them. I showed them my Jap battle flag and told them how the Seabees used to tear up bed sheets and spill mercurochrome on them to sell to suckers as Jap battle flags. But I had the real thing. The Seabee I bought mine from told me so. He also sold me a bottle of mercurochrome. He had several.

It made me feel like a big shot to tell everyone how I slept in Admiral Halsey's bed on Guadalcanal. But I didn't tell them I had to get up in the middle of the night to take off the rockers because I couldn't sleep. And I closed with a demonstration of a Japanese pistol I'd brought home.

I got out the gun and gave a short lecture on the dangers of playing with unloaded firearms. "They're sometimes loaded," I said. "You've got to be very sure they're empty before you pull the trigger." To demonstrate, I pulled and dug a junior-grade foxhole in the door of my closet. A moth stuck its head out and said, "What's all the shooting for, or are we on the wrong side?"

But to get back, it's sensational when you think of it. Not two years ago, 8000 miles in fifty hours seemed unbelievable. The same 8000 can now literally be done in half the time. And that's just the tag end of what war did to speed up aviation. But then, that's what war seems to be, progress by destruction.

Every war in history has given us something terrific. I suppose World War II's greatest contribution is control of the chain reaction, if we can control the control. The last war

So This Is Peace

introduced the control of the air. The Spanish War gave us control of yellow fever, and the Civil War gave us Scarlett O'Hara. I guess that makes the Civil War more glamorous. It really was our most "romantic" war. It certainly sounds that way when Bing tells us about it. Of course he was too old for anything but limited service.

But as younger men have our memories, too. I can remember the sunny days when transcontinental air travel started. And when it rained, it stopped. In those days, the trip from New York to Los Angeles was made in two Ford trimotor planes and the Hotel Muehlbach. The hotel never left Kansas City. You got away from New York in the morning in one of those big Ford corrugated-metal, trimotor jobs and spent the night in Kansas City. In the morning you left Kansas City and flew all day to Los Angeles. And as soon as you got to Los Angeles you left for the hospital.

There was no heat in the plane, no air conditioning, and no soundproofing. But it was worth it. You could make the coast-to-coast trip in thirty-nine hours and in another thirty-nine hours have back your normal hearing. Those trimotor planes were really impressive. They came in right after aerodynamic engineers abandoned the idea of propelling heavier-than-air craft with twisted rubber bands and decided to try motors, hence the name. There was a motor in each wing and a third motor in the nose. In those days experts agreed it was safer to have a motor in the nose. Naturally, when this theory was disproved, I had mine taken out, too. But it permanently altered the shape of my nose.

In the days of the trimotor plane, clippers were what the barber used to trim the back of your neck. Then came clippers to fly the ocean. Then came the Constellation and now clippers are what barbers use to trim the back of your neck.

Even that isn't so important since radar has made overwater flying so much safer for land planes. With radar and the automatic pilot, it's possible to select a spot and land on a pin point. But then, I had a teacher who used to do that every time she sat down. Then she'd grab hold of me and select a spot.

Right now Pan-American is flying Connies daily from Los Angeles and San Francisco to Honolulu. The trip is scheduled to take nine and one-half hours. It's been done in seven. That's considerably faster than the time it took us. But everyone knows even seven hours is slow compared to what the jet jobs will make it in. When they get those supersonic babies in regular passenger service, we'll be able to leave the Coconut Grove in Los Angeles in the middle of a rhumba and be in a coconut grove with a hula dancer in three shakes. Of course, this speed will take a lot of the easygoing beauty of sight-seeing out of flying. I'll never forget the first time, or the last, I flew to Honolulu. It was the same time. How restful it was to idle over the Golden Gate Bridge at a dreamy 200 miles per hour!

The plane they flew us to Hawaii in that summer of 1944 was a C-54 litter plane en route to Saipan to pick up some wounded. That meant for the trip to Pearl Harbor we were able to lie down and take it easy instead of sitting up for hours on end. And by "on end" I mean in one of those bucket seats. They may be all right for some people. But it's silly to ask a bucket to do a washtub job.

On that trip there were six of us, Frances Langford and Patty Thomas and the four nobody ever looked at. Patty joined our group for the purpose of studying the dance technique in the South Sea islands. There was a lot of dance technique studied, too. But guess who did the studying. Some of the guys even drooled for a little homework.

The four who didn't even get a sidewise glance for eight weeks were Old Brush-head Colonna; Tony Romano, hero of so many guitar solos; Barney Dean, who has tagged himself my personal jester so that he can tell people he's nobody's fool, and of course, the fourth member was Crosby's straight man. Everybody asked why we took Barney along, including Barney. The truth was we had him with us in case we had to trade with the natives. We tried to trade him three times, but the natives were too shrewd for us. They said *their* coconuts had more hair on them.

We started that tour of what was sometimes called the

Old Rocket Plane's Got Us

Sarong Circuit, and sometimes the Mosquito Network, at Pearl Harbor in 1944 and spent about nine days in the Hawaiian Islands. We didn't get a chance to play to all the men in the islands because some of them had work to do. Others heard we were coming and *found* work to do.

In those days the Hawaiian Islands were the Manhattan Transfer of the Pacific. They kept pumping men and supplies eastward and back. Along the same line of supply came the battle-scarred fighters to rest and recuperate in the many hospitals and playgrounds planned to wipe out some of the memory of the horror and grim monotony of Pacific Patrol.

And there were many different types of treatment administered by as many different physicians and nurses. But it was about Chaplain James Becker, whom we met on a flight from Oahu, that we heard the most wonderful stories. Jimmy Becker hated being attached to hospitals, where his main job was comforting the dying.

So in the hope of being transferred to more active duty, he started to louse up his hospital job. And lousing up a chaplain's job is really doing some top-flight lousing.

Becker's method to prove himself unfit for ward work was to walk up to a bed and say to the guy, "You're not sick at all. You look great." A few days after Jimmy started this technique, his CO congratulated him on how wonderfully he was handling the boys in the wards and how much faster they were recovering.

Jimmy, himself, told me about a malaria case. He was asked to administer last rites to an Air Force mechanic he'd flown with. Instead, Becker said, "You can't do this to your team, son. You're the best motor tuner in the whole Troop Carrier Command. You can't conk out! Now let's go."

The next day the CO told Jimmy the boy had perked up

and would live. The nurses tell me they were simply amazed at the brazenness of Chaplain James Becker's handling of the sick. But Becker got results. The nurses were amazed at my brazenness, too. But I didn't get results.

In Hawaii, at the time we were there, was Captain Maurice Evans of Special Services, the guy who humanized Hamlet for the GI's and then brought this idea to Broadway with smash results. Here was one of the world's finest actors so anxious to help us do our shows for the wounded men that he was carrying Barney Dean's bag. Fine thing; all Barney had in it were some old racing forms. Maurice Evans was really one of the unsung heroes of the Hawaiian Area. He was absolutely tireless in seeing that the men got an endless supply of the kind of entertainment they liked and wanted. He just wasn't interested in sleep. But we fixed that. He saw fifteen minutes of our show and slept soundly for two hours. I loved talking to Maurice. Those Shakespearean actors speak a different language. They have a Shakespearean quotation for everything. Their conversation's more Bard than a San Quentin window. I happened to mention Bing, and Evans murmured, "*'He doth nothing but talk of his horses.'*"

"Call those nags horses?"

"*'The best in his kind are but shadows,'*" Maurice answered. Then he said, "Say, when are we going to see that new picture you and Bing made with Dottie Lamour?" This proved he knew something besides Shakespeare.

"You like Dottie?" I asked.

He looked heavenward and murmured, "*'A dish for the gods.'*"

Then I asked him what he thought when he heard that Colonna and I were coming to Pearl, and he said, "*'Here come a pair of very strange beasts, which in all tongues are called fools.'"*

"Is that good or bad?" I asked.

"Bob," said Evans, "*'I'd rather have a fool to make me merry than a wise man to make me sad.'*"

"Just what does that really mean?"

"It explains why Jack Benny has a bigger Hooperating than Mr. Anthony."

Also among the Army personnel helping to entertain the men was Joe DiMaggio, who pitched for the Seventh Air Force's ball team. Those fliers had a pretty good club, featuring such men as Joe Gordon and Bill Dickey. But then the Army had a fair system for getting good ball teams. They had a man named Hershey in charge of it.

All told, we did about thirty-five shows in the islands, for about 100,000 men. And we finished each show by saying, "If there's anything you don't like about our show we'd like to have you all tell us."

All told.

CHAPTER 4

Back to Abnormal, See?

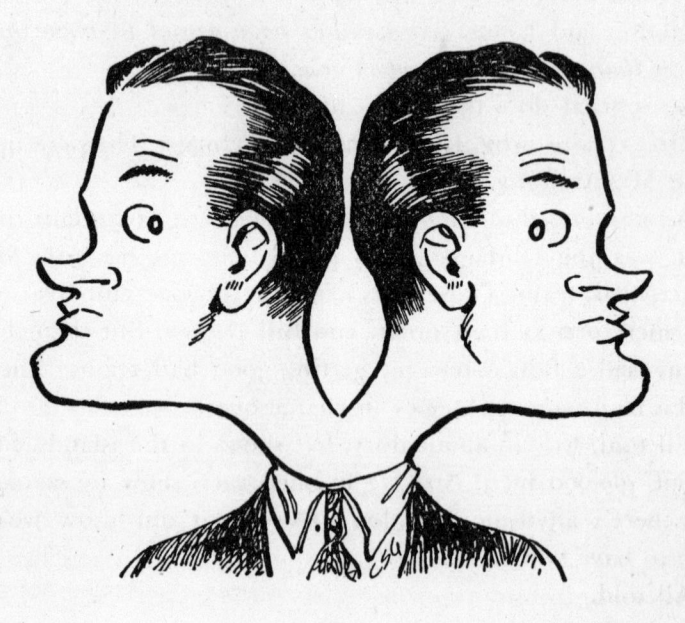

As soon as V-J Day turned into yesterday, everybody started talking about what nobody has yet called N-Day—that certain day when we were all suddenly and miraculously supposed to be "back to normal."

In all our postwar travels we were always finding different groups of people fighting for what they called "normal." Normal being what *they* wanted. They didn't see anything unusual in that. But the group they were fighting always called them a pressure group. One Navy nurse I first met in Honolulu and talked to again in Des Moines told me her only beef about all the pressure groups was that there were so many of them a housewife still couldn't walk into a store and buy a pressure cooker. Pressure cooker, that's a pot that

Back to Abnormal, See?

only takes two minutes to cook your vegetables and blow the roof off your house.

Dolores tells me you can cook peas in a pressure cooker almost as fast as you can open a can. She says the fast-cooking steam seals in the vitamins. I always thought vitamins came from pills. The pressure cooker, I'm told, is just a postwar discovery that proves how unhealthful old-fashioned cooking was. It was so bad I'm actually afraid to eat a pie like Mother used to make. And I was afraid to eat it when Mother used to make it. The only thing Mother ever cooked successfully was Father's goose.

Next to a pressure cooker—that's Hope with a safety valve—the things the gals like best are their deep-freeze units. They're really wonderful and a big improvement on the refrigerator. It took women a long time to become emancipated from the icebox and the nuisance of that steady drip on the back porch. Then came the electric refrigerator and those long lonesome mornings. Now with the deep freeze, everything is back to normal. Just as the icebox worked only if the iceman came every day, the deep-freeze unit works only if the appliance man comes every day. And the finance man once a week.

But the average GI won't have any trouble with the gadgets that go into a modern home. If he can find the door they go into. I got a load of one of those round Dymaxion houses in Kansas City. In case you haven't seen one, they're like a merry-go-round and instead of having a foundation they're suspended from a center pole like a tent. The outer, circular wall is practically all glass. This is fine to let in sunlight. But there's always the question whether the age of the Atomic Bomb is the ideal time to live in a glass house.

The only really bad feature of the round house is that all

So This Is Peace

the rooms, including the bedroom, are wedge-shaped like a piece of pie. And it seems to me psychologically wrong for newlyweds to start their honeymoon in a triangle.

Luckily, not all the postwar houses are round. Some are square, some are oblong, and some are flat. But all have new stuff. Some of the new homes in the Southwest feature what they call solar heating. That's just a fancy name for getting the sun to heat your house for you. But my father had that idea in Cleveland years ago when he took me down in the cellar and handed me a coal shovel. Some people also keep their homes cool by having a few inches of running water on the roof. Many Los Angeles homes added this feature last year during the flood season. They even had a few inches of running water in the cellar.

Naturally, these ultramodern houses have to have ultramodern furniture to fit them. And the furniture doesn't only have to fit the house. The new idea is that it has to fit the occupant. In Grand Rapids I saw some of the new furniture suites. They're designed exactly like bathing suits, to fit the curves of the body. But they have their disadvantages. A guy like Sydney Greenstreet might sit on a chair designed for Betty Grable and get up a mass of accordion pleats.

But I've got to admit the new furniture's comfortable. The springs are deeper, the cushions are wider and softer, the joinings and materials are more resilient . . . everything seems to give more, including the guy who pays the bill. Modern furniture designers claim they've finally found out how to adapt all the angles of carpentry to the curves of the body. And I've got to admit that any man who can sell what looks like a lacquered orange crate for $250 knows his angles.

I saw the last word in modern furniture when I got home to Hollywood. We have a store that specializes in upholstered

Back to Abnormal, See?

pianos. I wouldn't care to say that these are for people who prefer soft music. But I *would* like to point out that while upholstering baby grands may be strictly a postwar thing in Hollywood, our dressmakers have been upholstering grand babies for years. But to get back to normal:

Ever since 1921 and Warren G. Harding, we've been *hoping* to "get back to normalcy." So the 1946 version consisted of two groups. One group said go this way; one said go that way. One said save. The other said spend. Naturally, my sympathies were with the group that favored saving. But I liked to go out to dinner with the spenders.

While the two groups were arguing, the people began to realize they didn't have any desire to "get back to normal." I know that what my parents thought was normal certainly isn't what people today consider normal. My parents thought *I* was normal.

Normal, before the war, was at least two hundred miles an hour slower than it is today. Today everything is bigger and faster.

But along with all the speed and comfort the airways are offering at attractive prices, there's plenty of cause for worry. The railroads have the cause. And they've started to fight back.

It took the keen competition after a global war to get them to operate through Pullman service from coast to coast. Formerly you couldn't get through Chicago without changing cars unless you were a cow, and too often they routed the cows through the Stock Yards. But now there's no more changing cars in the Windy City, which means Chicago cab drivers are going to have to be satisfied with just killing Chicagoans.

As soon as the railroads got that kid out of Upper Seven,

they saw the smoke-writing in the sky and the Greyhounds on the road. Pullman began to get competition from Budd, and the pictures and prices of railroad accommodations in the ads made people suffering from the housing shortage try to get a two-year lease on a compartment on the Super-Chief.

No kidding, the new sleeping cars are so big they're equipped with scooters to take you to the diner. And everything tucks into something. I've been on one of those fancy new cars. Open one thing and it's a bed. Open another thing and it's a washstand. Open a third thing and . . . oops!

I found this out on a recent trip to the Monterey Peninsula with Dolores and the two kids. It was the first time we'd all been out together in so long; none of us knew how to act. The first morning at the Lodge I came in for breakfast after a fast nine holes in the fog, and the two kids were already at table. As I entered, Tony hollered across the dining room, "Good morning, Bob Hope."

Naturally, everyone started to laugh.

So I said, "Look, that 'Bob Hope' stuff is okay when we're alone. But when we're out in public, just call me Daddy. If you don't mind!"

And Linda said, "We know, Daddy, we'll let *you* get the laughs!"

I would never take a thing like that except from a relative. Of course, it's getting so that every place I turn there are relatives. But half the joy of my last trip to England was the anticipation of seeing them. I crossed on the *Queen Mary*. (Came back via Pan-American Clipper. I didn't want to make the trip both ways by rail.) I won't say we had a rough crossing, but fish kept following the boat, begging for seasick pills. I didn't have any to spare.

It was 1945. Half the war'd been won and we had Tojo

Back to Abnormal, See?

reeling. The last time I'd sailed on the *Queen Mary* was in 1939. We were on the high seas, en route to America, the day Hitler marched into Poland. The *Queen* was a luxury liner in those days and the trip was as smooth as Crosby's scalp. But traveling exclusively with GI's for five years is enough to make any queen rough.

We boarded the *Queen* at 9 P.M. and were told by the colonel in charge of the United States Army Military Personnel that once aboard we couldn't get off. "You're our prisoners now," he said impishly, and disappeared.

We hadn't been on that boat ten minutes when we got the scuttlebutt that she wasn't sailing until five the next morning. So there we were, only three miles from such centers of New York culture as the Stork Club, El Morocco, and "21." We could almost see them waving their cover charges at us. So we looked up this colonel who had said we were his prisoners and said, "Who's running this ship? You or the British?"

This hit him right in his dignity, and he said, "I am in charge of military personnel."

So we told him we thought that made him a big enough man to let us get off. "It just can't be done," he said. "Never *has* been done!"

I pleaded with him . . . even told him we'd left some lyrics to a very important song at Leon and Eddie's. He looked me right in the eye and answered, "The purser wants to see you for a dash and a splash." I told him all we wanted was to dash and as far as we were concerned the purser could go splash.

But the colonel won, and for half an hour we threw a few accents back at the British in the purser's cabin. And when we came out there was our friend the colonel waiting for us, with passes. "Just show these and keep moving," he said. We did. The shavetail at the head of the gangplank almost fell overboard when he saw it.

The boat sailed on schedule at five. But we were floating by midnight.

The first day out I spoke to Commodore Sir James Bisset, commander of the *Queen*. Two days later we were introduced and he spoke to me. What a guy! He was sixty-three and constantly on duty for five years, carrying men and equipment through mine fields, past submarine wolf packs, and under the wings of Jerry divebombers, without mishap. Then he found me aboard.

Naturally, after we met, I worked it so I got to sit at the captain's table, except at mealtime.

Back to Abnormal, See?

But it was a thrilling crossing and symbolic of everything we fought for—Wendell Wilkie's One World. The greatest liner afloat, a British boat, was heading for Europe to bring home thousands of American doggies and deliver, among other widely assorted elements of the human race, a bunch of RAF fliers who'd been training in Texas; some Russian and Polish Army officers; some German PW's; a couple of battalions of Japanese-American replacements to relieve high-point combat men; a few English citizens who'd just been released by American soldiers from a Manila concentration camp; some American civilians on government business; and our troupe that looked like nobody's business. The *Queen* was sort of a United Nations conference with a purser.

And Frank McHugh, who made a trip home from Germany on the *Queen* shortly after V-E Day, told me something about that purser. Frank says the purser had been told by the captain that he wanted to read *Forever Amber* and ordered him to get a copy of the book. The purser had forgotten.

How a man could forget *Forever Amber,* I don't know. But when the purser told Frank how close he was to the doghouse, McHugh said, "If the captain really wants a copy of *Forever Amber,* I will give him mine in return for a fresh-water bath." Frank said he really needed that fresh-water "tub," having been in salt water so much he was beginning to grow green warts like a dill pickle.

Later I asked Frank why he was running around Europe carrying a big volume like *Forever Amber.*

"Kept my shirts in it," he said. "It kept them from getting wrinkled."

McHugh had another yarn about his European tour. His

troupe was in a little town about fourteen miles behind the lines during the Battle of the Bulge. In the middle of the night Frank suddenly heard rifle fire. He awoke with a start and as he listened, machine guns started popping . . . then a few mortars opened up, and Frank's blood turned to jellied Madrilène. I know the feeling well.

After wondering what to do, thinking the Germans had broken through, and realizing if this were the case nothing was the right thing to do . . . he finally did the wrong thing. He went to the window, opened it, exposing himself to all kinds of gunfire, and looked out. Immediately a GI looked up and hollered at him. He hollered, "Happy New Year!"

Only the other day, when I met Marlene Dietrich on the lot at Paramount, her immaculate self again, I thought how she had slogged all over Europe for five years, entertaining the boys. Marlene tells me that peace has forced her to get conditioned all over again to what we know as modern conveniences. She told me she'd been back six months before she started looking around for signs reading "Powder Room" instead of searching for a nurse or WAC to ask the all-important question. It is certainly apropos that her first role should be that of a gypsy in Paramount's *Golden Earrings*, in which she plays the daughter of a French Bourbon and as usual Ray Milland is the stepchild of straight rye.

But on the subject of conveniences I like Mary Brian's story about the answer to the $64 question, "Where is it?" Mary was jeepbound through the French countryside to play a show. The section was not only primitive, it didn't even have one of those. So Mary discreetly had them stop the jeep while she went on an enforced daisy hunt. She had hardly disappeared from view when an American infantry sergeant began firing an automatic rifle to attract her attention and

Back to Abnormal, See?

screamed "Hey, Miss, get out of there! We haven't gone over that ground with the vacuum cleaners yet."

Mary came leaping from behind the tree, a bunch of EM's with mine detectors made an elaborate sweep around the area, then the sergeant doffed his helmet graciously to Miss Brian and said, "Now, Miss!"

But to get back to the *Queen Mary*. Many thousands of GI's have a soft spot in their hearts for her and her sister ship, the *Queen Elizabeth*. Those two boats brought back 15,000 men at a clip. And it was possible to get clipped, too. The boats roll just enough so that you don't have to wear out the dice.

But we got even for the dough we lost, making them listen to our rehearsals. Only we didn't tell anyone they were rehearsals. We didn't have to. We did a very polite show the first night out for the other civilians aboard the ship, the officers and the Army brass, in the Grand Salon.

Then we did a second show in the dining saloon for the enlisted personnel who like an extra *o* in their "salon." Naturally, we had to do a third show for the guys who were on duty and couldn't catch the second show. Then we found out that there were a bunch of men aboard for whom we'd played in Honolulu and they hadn't been asked to see the show. So we did a special show for them. We practically did a show in every cabin on the boat, a whole week of vaudeville booking at sea.

All of which was very lucky because our friend the colonel was so pleased with all the shows he helped us through customs very fast. We left the *Queen* at a little town in Scotland called Gourock. I shouldn't say that's what it was called. That's what it was gargled. When a Scot pronounces Gourock he sounds as if he had a frog in his throat and the frog had a chill.

As soon as we set foot ashore Colonel MacNicol of the POE at Gourock took care of us. POE . . . now that we're at peace again they've put the letter B back in front of it and it means Elk. But during the war POE meant Port of Embarkation.

Colonel MacNicol handed us our railroad tickets through to Southampton, boat tickets to Le Harve, and plane tickets to Paris. It was all set. But not according to the plans I had in mind. I wanted to go to London to see my folks. The Savoy was calling me. So I said to MacNicol, "How do we get to Prestwick to get a plane to London?"

He looked at me the way the colonel on the boat had when I said we wanted to get off. There were no orders to send us to Prestwick. No orders to fly us from Prestwick to London. But MacNicol had heard about the shows we'd done on the *Queen* and wanted to help. All he could think of to say, however, was, "What are we going to do, Bob? Prestwick's a hundred miles away."

Back to Abnormal, See?

I said, "We won the war. We must have an extra car." And I was right. There was one. We finally settled with Jerry and me on our way to Prestwick, and Colonel Mac making arrangements to get the rest of the troupe on the train for London.

When we arrived in Prestwick I knew my way around. I'd been stranded there before. It was the 42nd Street and Broadway of wartime air travel and is still the Mecca of all golfers. Well, to most golfers it's Mecca. But my game always had more of a Cubeb quality. For years I thought the green grass on the fairways was just for cows. I found out later it was for actors waiting for their options to be picked up.

I went right to the office of Colonel Spake, the CO of the Prestwick operation, and said, "I want to go to London."

He said, "Say hello, first."

So I said hello and he told me it was impossible to get me out. I said, "I've got Jerry with me."

"I haven't even got *two* seats!" the colonel said.

"I'll hold Jerry on my lap," I said. "It'll only cost me half fare. I always take Colonna with me wherever I fly. It gets chilly sometimes and his mustache keeps me warm."

"Forget about getting out of here," Spake urged, "and play a little golf."

"Jerry and I played the last time I was here," I told him. "And I won't say the grounds were in bad condition but I thought I'd made a hole-in-one until a gopher handed me back my ball." I didn't have my golf things with me that time either. Luckily I always play in my bare feet. There's nothing in the rules that says you can't carry a spare ball between your toes.

We really played badly that time at Prestwick. Our caddie

was a little Scottish lad, and I felt sorry for him. He was in the woods so long he came out with a tail.

While I was dreaming, Colonel Spake disappeared. They told me he'd gone home. So I went to his house and this time I really started to talk. And I got my usual results. I've had doors slammed in my face before. How do you think my nose got its upsweep? So I opened the door again, told the Colonel he couldn't intimidate a civilian, and walked right into his living room. Then I got up and dusted myself off and walked right into his living room. Then I got up and dusted myself off and walked right into his living room. Those Texans are persistent and they can throw anything. And Colonel Spake was really a solid callus from Dallas. But when I got through with him, or vice versa, I had the callus.

So I looked up Alec Templeton and let him play to me to soothe my ruffled nerves. It's nice soothing. Alec was on his way home from tossing a mess of music at the ETO and when Alec tosses music it's no mess. He's one of the most miraculous musicians I know and one of the nicest guys. If I had his mind I wouldn't talk to myself, I'd be so proud.

Back to Abnormal, See?

While I was sitting there listening to Alec play, Colonel Spake suddenly appeared, stood right in front of us, and then Spake spoke.

He said there were about 1400 combat fliers with flights of B-24's and B-17's waiting to go stateside for some rest and reconversion to the bigger four-motored jobs scheduled to do most of the pagoda busting around Yokohama and it would be great if we did a show for these guys.

I won't say I drive a shrewd bargain, but I said, "It would be great if we did a show if you had a C-47 with the motors running waiting to take us to London after the show."

Colonel Spake held a quick conference with some other officers and then said, "It's a deal."

I said, "Start the motors."

So Alec, Jerry, and I hit them with all we had. Alec played the piano. Jerry sang and played the trombone. And I just stood there and ducked. The way that Templeton played. After the show I couldn't resist grabbing his hand and saying, "Alec, you certainly are an artist."

Then he gave my hand a cordial squeeze and said, "Good-by."

Naturally, as soon as we had our C-47 waiting for us we all became very popular with a lot of other people who were willing to go to London for one reason or another.

One of our fellow passengers was Ann Hathaway, a blue-eyed Red Cross girl who looked like a fugitive from Varga. I say she was a fellow passenger, but when I threw my arm around her shoulder and said, "Hya, fella!" she changed my mind.

Ann, like so many wonderful Red Cross gals, had been in the ETO for several years, peddling crullers to our guys from a Clubmobile. She had great respect for our doughfoots'

So This Is Peace

ability to stow doughnuts. But I figure any guy'd come back for a second sinker just to grab another close-up of Ann.

Someday the whole story of courage and self-sacrifice on the part of Red Cross girls all over the world is going to be written. When it is, I hope the author can do justice to his marvelous subject.

There was one really sad person on that flight down to London, our pilot, 1st Lt. Roy Cooley. It seemed he was slated for Uncle Sugar, but he still had a face as long as Crosby's feed bill. I said, "If you're headed home, why are you sad?"

"I'm only a lieutenant," he said.

"What's wrong with that?" I asked.

"I'm from Lexington, Kentucky, and every man in town's a colonel."

But he landed us safely through his tears, and by the time I got my room at the Savoy, it was almost 11 P.M. and not quite dark. July nights are so short in London, burglars work by appointment only.

Seeing London for the first time since 1943 was really amazing. The changes were tremendous. Many of the scars left by the blitz had already begun to disappear. The lights were on again. John Watts of BBC arranged a delightful twilight cruise up the Thames in a police boat with an inspector of police to point out damage done by buzz bombs. I asked one bobby who was helping to run the boat what seemed to be most different about London with the European war over.

"Well, guvnor," he said, "the most different thing I'd say is that there seems to be almost as many Englishmen on the streets now as Americans."

First thing the next morning I drove down to Hitchin to see my relatives.

Back to Abnormal, See?

In case you still haven't read *I Never Left Home*, * that really is where my folks lived when my father left home for the United States. It's a typical little English village, the kind you expect to see a calendar under. Little shoppes and pubs line the streets that stagecoaches used to go through to the sound of cracking whips. In 1945, jeeps were still going through to the sound of cracking bones.

When I arrived in Hitchin all my family was home. They didn't know was coming. But they were gracious and started to get tea ready. It wasn't the same without my grandfather, though. And there was a slight accident. I heard someone say, "Cousin Albert, please put the pot on the stove," and before I could stop him he scorched my pants.

---

* PUBLISHER'S NOTE: Price $2.00 in cloth, $1.00 in paper. Get your copy at once. You may be the reason for a new printing.

So This Is Peace

After tea we took the traditional sight-seeing trip around Hitchin and once more they showed me the building that was built in 1100 and is still in use.

That evening we went back to London to do a big Fourth of July show in Albert Hall for 10,000 GI's. Albert Hall's sort of like Carnegie in New York and the Philharmonic in Los Angeles. They usually hold only concerts and such things there, so naturally the manager was worried about our kind of show going on in his hall. I heard him arguing with an MP, but he finally let us do the show when he was told that the United States Army would pay half of the fumigating expenses.

Next morning I took a cab to Buckingham Palace. It was on that taxi ride that I understood how Londoners developed the stamina to carry them through the blitz. They were toughened up riding in London taxis. Those old cabs look like something the Smithsonian Institution turned down. They're so high the doorman can't just help you out. He has to wait till the driver lowers a rope ladder.

Driving through St. James's Park I noticed that the sheep were grazing as they had for hundreds of years. But they may have put a stop to that by now because of the food shortage. . . . Even in 1945, the people were complaining that the sheep ate all the grass. Really, food was so scarce that London was the only place in the world where "man bites dog" wasn't news.

And it got worse in 1946. One year after the war ended, England got its first sample of bread rationing. While we fought over whether or not to keep on OPA-ing, Great Britain and all of Europe worried how they could keep on EATing. We got rid of food rationing and they prayed for some food to ration. They carried on in spite of big shortages, and every small shortage we came up against really

Back to Abnormal, See?

made *us* carry on. We sent Herbert Hoover over to investigate the food situation. And when he brought in his report half of us said he was wrong and asked for too little. The other half claimed he was wrong and asked for too much. And we all passed our plates and asked for more.

We even griped because liquor was scarce. And when it began to look as if we might need a doctor's prescription to get the real bonded stuff, W. C. Fields started paying top prices for good, clean germs.

I wouldn't say W. C. drinks to excess. But recently he offered to donate some blood to the Red Cross Civilian Blood Bank and his plasma had an olive in it. But whenever

I start to worry about the food situation in the U. S. A., I just think of Frank Sinatra and Bing Crosby. In what other country could a hunk of spaghetti and a meat ball wind up with so much gravy? Which reminds me that the State Department is keeping Frankie a secret. Just a couple of months ago we sent his picture to Europe, and now they're sending us food.

But let's face it, nobody in show business has done a more sincere job of fighting for what he feels is right than Frankie. He toured Italy, singing for the GI's, and he's been tireless in talking against intolerance, bigotry, and the causes of juvenile delinquency. And the causes aren't always what we think they are.

The high school and college kids in their hopped-up hotrods, that everyone complained about before the war, turned out to be the "hot fighter pilots" who made a blow-joe out of Tojo and wafted the "luft" out of the Luftwaffe.

We have a problem of what to do with the younger generation of that bunch that's growing up right now. The city of Los Angeles hates to pinch the hop-ups who race their hotrods with souped-up mills, but the squirrels in the gookwagons who peel-off on L. A.'s public highways are actually a menace.

If you don't collar that lingo it's just the squirrel-jive you can dig in a drive-in called Piccadilly Circus near Sepulveda and Culver Blvds. in L. A. where squirrels have found a happy piece of highway on which to lay aside their binders.

In an article about hop-ups and their rigs I read that, "Nobody seems to know just why southern California should have given birth to the hot-rod craze." Obviously the writer never drove a car in Los Angeles traffic. In London, traffic moves on the left side of the street. In Detroit it moves on the right side of the street. In Los Angeles it moves in the middle of the street, both ways . . . but *moves!*

The same article says that the reason a squirrel gets the urge to ignore the binders, burn his boots, heat up his mill and lay a strip down some lonesome road is California's "year-round good weather, six-lane superhighways, or a stock of old cars that is abundant in comparison with other sections of the country." It's certainly true about the abundance of old cars. A Stevens-Duryea with a high wax job gets billed as a late model in most L. A. used-car parks. But what good are the six-lane highways when they're filled six abreast with these old cars, many of them driven by men and women whose driving is as varicose as their veins? And as for the year-round good weather, the most consistent weather southern California has had in the past ten years is whether to carry an umbrella or whether to believe the Chamber of Commerce.

But to get back to hot-rods, they're generally 1928 to 1938 roadsters . . . or whatever model was available, skinned down to roadster lines. But any old car whittled down to its essential ugliness isn't a hot-rod. You can cut off the top of a car, strip off the fenders, lose the windshield, put on goggles, and push it as fast as you can heat it up, but you won't be handling a hot-rod. You'll be operating what the hot-rod boys call a gook-wagon, a crock, a goat, or a crutch. In fact, so you'll be able to go back and understand what's been said so far, here's the complete glossary of hop-up hot-rod lingo.

HOT-ROD, RIG, OUTFIT, HOT-IRON—Any fast, stripped-down stock model car that's been doctored by a hop-up.

HOP-UP—Anybody, man, woman or child (and many are), who tinkers with an automobile to materially increase its speed.

GOOK-WAGON—A snappy, chrome-trimmed, noisy, belligerent stock car cut down to look like a hot-rod but lacking any speed refinements to put it in competition with the solid rigs.

SQUIRREL—High-school-age owner of a gook-wagon, crock, goat, or crutch; any driver of any pitiful imitation of a hot-rod.

STACKS—Exhaust pipes. Like gals who like to ride in them, a good hot-rod is generally very elaborately stacked.

POTS, JUGS—Carburetors. A very fast hot-iron sometimes has two or three pots.

SLUGS—Pistons.

DRAG, PEEL-OFF, LAY A STRIP—To pick up speed rapidly, really get away.

BINDERS—Brakes.

BOOTS—Tires.

MILL—Engine.

A hop-up would as soon call a goat a jalopy as he'd tag a slick-chick a flapper. Jalopy is a word of another era. And the era of the hot-rod has its origin obscured by lack of historians. One man's guess is as good as another's, with many hating to guess. But most people who are interested in the development of the hot-rod think it's a carry-over from the old Tin Lizzie daze when there actually *were* flappers, and jalopies were the queens of the road. Surely it was in those days between wars when the kids got motor-minded. Until today, as the old saying goes, "a boy's best friend is his motor."

I've gotten a load of some of those hopped-up goats, while playing in college towns. And I must admit some of the kids do seem to overdo it. I won't say what one kid was using for

Back to Abnormal, See?

fuel, but every ten miles he had to stop and blow the foam off his carburetor.

One freshman hopped up his motor so much it always ran six blocks ahead of the car. I'd hate to say he had his motor too souped up, but it was the first time I ever saw a car backfiring noodles.

But those squirrels take good care of their gook-wagons. Sometimes they'll spend a whole day washing, waxing, and shining them and then spend the evening marcelling the beaver tail tied to the radiator cap. I say beaver tail. They tell me they're really fox tails. But what would an eager beaver be doing with a fox's tail?

Another wonderful thing about those hopped-up cars is the number of people they'll carry. I was riding with a Stanford sophomore, and the rest of his class, through Palo Alto one Tuesday afternoon, and he heard a rattle in his engine. When he lifted the hood, there were three freshmen shooting craps.

But some of the kids go too far. I saw one frosh sitting in a Ford without a motor. So I said "How can you drive without a motor?" And a coed stuck her head out and said, "Who's driving, and mind your own business."

I really don't think the automobile or anything connected with the war that isn't a psychological wound, or a broken-up family, has anything to do with juvenile delinquency. Children who were neglected may be wild and sometimes, I guess, the neglect can be attributed to the war. But that theory, "they gave him a gun" and so his trigger finger itches, sounds kind of farfetched to me. No one says, "Don't teach a man electronics and radar" because it will contribute to his downfall.

There is delinquency, juvenile and otherwise, in the wake of every war, and one psychologist—an Englishman, I think—said that juvenile delinquency was really only children trying to do what their parents do.

There's an awful lot of worrying about postwar morals. And it goes pretty far. I read in the paper the other day that "the ladies of the Humane Education League are distressed by the number of unwanted puppies roaming the streets." And they don't mean the frankfurters in those traveling hot-dog wagons.

The ladies met in solemn session and drew up a petition demanding a municipal morals code for canines. The ladies say in their petition that "promiscuous backyard breeding is responsible for thousands of unwanted puppies running loose." It seems loose dogs result in loose dogs, an odd case of cause and effect being identical.

The ladies actually want the city to, as they say, "keep pets in line with propriety." Now comes the problem of how to keep silly ladies with nothing better to do than worry

Back to Abnormal, See?

about the dalliance of dogs "in line with propriety." As for the dogs, the best way to keep them in line is just keep them on a line.

I don't know what the dog problem in England is, but I doubt if they're worrying much about it if there's anything like the juvenile-delinquency problem I'm told there is. And I'm sure they'll resolve their j. d. problem as easily as they've taken so much punishment in the past ten years from both within and without. The English people have really had it. Yet they continue to wear their problems with a typically casual courage and, in the face of everything, maintain their nonchalance. They never lose their *savoir-faire*. The men still carry canes and wear their handkerchiefs in their sleeves. Of course I tried to do it, too. But my box of Kleenex made too big a bulge.

I also tried talking the way my English relatives do. And you know, it isn't easy talking without using your mouth. It seems when I talk through my nose my words turn somersaults.

So This Is Peace

Of course, London, being the home of the Well-Dressed Man, Crosby created quite a furor. He strolled through Piccadilly, and people followed him the way children chased the Pied Piper through the streets of Hamlin. Yes, sir, those pipes of Bing's—and I don't mean the ones he smokes—had a magical effect on morale wherever he showed up. And he showed up wherever there was a guy in uniform because every one of those GI's carried Crosby in his heart. Nobody gave more of his time and talent to the AFRS and nobody came anywhere near as close to being a real Ambassador of Good Will as did Der Bingle, who sang their folk songs in French to the French people and "I'm Dreaming of a White Christmas" in German to the Krauts—smacking the Heinie morale right where it was weakest—their ability to take it any longer. Wherever Bing went in London crowds gathered and had to be dispersed by the bobbies.

The reason the constabulary had to disperse crowds when Bing was in London was because the city was still blacked out. It was before V-E Day and all large gatherings of any kind had to be broken up. One night Bing ducked down to a little restaurant in Soho for a midnight snack, and before he'd blown three choruses of "Blues in the Night" to cool his broth, there was a mob outside hollering for him.

A constable came in and said, "Igh sigh, sir, you 'ad better go to the window, sir, an' show your bloomin' fice."

So Bing went to the window and the crowd started screaming:

" 'Ow's for a song?"

"Sing something!"

"Sing for us."

"We wants to 'ear you sing!"

Back to Abnormal, See?

Bing said, "If I knock one number for you will you break it up and let me hang on the feed bag?"

"Right you are, guvnor!" a cockney hollered.

"What would you like to hear?"

The same cockney looked up and hollered, "If it ayn't too much trouble, guvnor, 'ow's for singin' your theme song . . . 'Thanks for the Memory'?"

CHAPTER 5

Don't You Know There's a Peace On?

WITH everybody picketing everyone for wanting to make a little extra money, and everybody accusing everybody else of keeping the peace from paying off, it's worked out so that we still go into restaurants, stores, and markets with that hopeless, shamefaced expression we had during rationing, and whisper, "Can I have a pound of butter?" as if we were asking for a bindle of snow. We do this because from the middle of 1942 to the middle of 1945 we found out that there was absolutely no good answer to a sharply spoken, "Don't you know there's a war going on?"

Little Mitzi Mayfair, who, with Carole Landis, Martha Raye, and Kay Francis, was one of the first so-called "soldiers in grease paint," ran into that routine at a point where it hurt most.

Mitzi had been playing in England, Iceland, and Scotland. And after three or four months of this pioneering, she followed the troops to North Africa, where she sprung an ulcer on one of her rear choppers. Her faced puffed out like an empty popcorn bag, and if you've ever tried tap dancing with an ulcerated tooth, let me tell you it's no fun. I happen to have had a little experience dancing with an ulcerated tooth. She left me with an ulcerated toe.

They tried to get Mitzi to go home, but she didn't want to quit. But no matter how game you are, you can stand only so much. And she finally had to start the long, painful trip home to the dentist. The flight across the Atlantic was rugged. They landed her in the South and the flight north was rugged. She had to hang around the Philadelphia airport before she finally got to share a seat on the plane going west with a Marine combat flier. And that was *really* rugged! Mitzi told him she thought she'd have to have her tooth pulled and he told her about how tough the Marines in his squadron were. "Wherever we have to have a tooth taken out," he said, "we just climb in the chair, point to the tooth, hand the dentist a wrench handle, and say, 'Contact!'"

But those Marine fliers are great guys. At one spot in the South Pacific, one hero of about sixty missions taxied around for five hours, trying to get his machine off the ground. He couldn't figure out why it wouldn't develop enough speed to take off until he found out his medals were dragging.

Finally Mitzi's plane was grounded in Texas. It was the weather, not the Marine's medals. By that time Mitzi had tried everything on her tooth but a plug of Mule Cut and a Hot Seabee. And there they were in the middle of nowhere. She began to think of all those nice comfortable jeep rides across the cool North African desert . . . of the guys she'd left in their cheerful airy foxholes . . . and she walked into the commissary of the airport to get some ice cream.

"Did you ask me for ice cream?" the waitress asked. And threw her a look that would have floored Joe Louis.

"Is there anything wrong with ordering ice cream?" Mitzi asked politely.

The girl just put her hands on her hips, looked at the gal who'd just flown about 10,000 miles from a battle front, with a screaming toothache, and said, "Listen, sister, don't you know there's a war on?"

But, of course, peace changed all that. You don't go into a restaurant any more and have a waiter insult you by reminding you there's a war on as the reason why he can't bring you any butter. You don't need the butter. There's no bread! The waiters, however, have become more polite. Now it's the customers who are saying, "Don't you know there's a peace going on?"

How long it'll keep going on is any man's guess, with electronic controls, atomic rays, and atomic bombs. No kidding, one high hunk of Army brass tabbed the length of the next war at forty minutes.

The one consoling thought is: if there's got to be a war, the short kind of war is the best. I know, because I've checked with the veterans who fought for the five freedoms . . . freedom of speech . . . freedom from want . . . freedom from fear . . . freedom of worship . . . and freedom from the Army. I'm speaking of the men who really sweated out the "point system" . . . that's Army slang for "Don't be so nervous, we'll tell you when to stop saluting." And don't get the idea the guys didn't stop doing that the moment they were handed their discharges. That's what they called the slip of paper that changed a man's name from "Colonel" to "Stinky."

I'll never forget the first visit I made to a camp where high-point men were waiting their separation from service. "How's this discharge system working out?" I asked.

"Great," a guy said, without any hesitation. "Things here

are moving along so well that any day now they may start letting out the men from *this* war."

Of course some officers did leave the service with regrets. That's what a lieutenant commander feels when he walks into his bank and finds that the vice-president is a former sailor he used to call "Stupid." And speaking of the Navy, there was a time when the discharge-points quota for the Navy changed so often they began installing ticker tape in every hammock.

Actually, once the war ended, the anxiety of some men to get enough points to leave the service was sometimes pitifully serious. Often at night you could hear sobbing. It was generally some officer who had enough points to get out if he were still a private.

Of course some veterans simply couldn't get enough points to get out. But I know of one lucky guy who just got under the wire as his wife presented him with a ten-point bouncing baby boy!

This couldn't happen to the younger men. And some of the veterans in the separation center were so young that when they were handed their discharge papers, the last paragraph said: "Greetings—you're drafted again."

In all my traveling around the country and in Europe after the war, I met only one bunch of guys who wanted to stay in uniform. But the uniform they wanted to stay in was Napoleon's. Any guy who thinks he has a beef because it took him a long time to get out by the point system should remember that Eisenhower isn't out yet!

In Paris, quite a while after V-J Day, I met a bunch of fliers who still went on practice missions. Every morning they held a big mass meeting to pick a volunteer to go tell the CO that the war was over!

So This Is Peace

But at least they were in Paris... City of Light. That means if you gave them a cigarette they'd supply the light. Or is Rome the City of Light? Can't be! You can't even get a match there!

We headed for Paris in the middle of July, 1945, by flying down from London to Tidworth, England, where we'd done a show in 1943. But so many things happened since then, they'd forgotten about us. At Tidworth we laid a little comic relief on the 44th Division, which had been a New York National Guard outfit. They'd taken it pretty rough, and were waiting to be redeployed to the Pacific. But even that kind of duty didn't get them out of seeing our show.

From Tidworth we hopped to Grove, where I ran into one of my postwar plans, a helicopter. That's sort of a Mixmaster that goes up. I *must* have one. Our pilot really gave me that "One World" feeling. He was Captain Herb Langdon, who lives two doors from me in North Hollywood. We had quite a talk on the way to Grove and I finally promised faithfully to return his lawn mower.

The 302nd Transport Wing of the Royal Air Force was stationed at Grove and they were the ones who had a few Lend-Lease helicopters. RAF Squadron Leader B. H. Arkell invited Colonna and me to take a ride and before we knew it we were going up like a yo-yo with jet propulsion. Helicopter, that's an elevator that's graduated from ground school. They're amazing! I mean the way they go straight up and hover. I hadn't experienced anything like it since my first hotfoot.

What a plane! You can fly right along and then stop dead outside a six-story window. Right then and there I made plans to own my own portable keyhole.

I had a happy surprise at Biggin Field when I got a gander

91

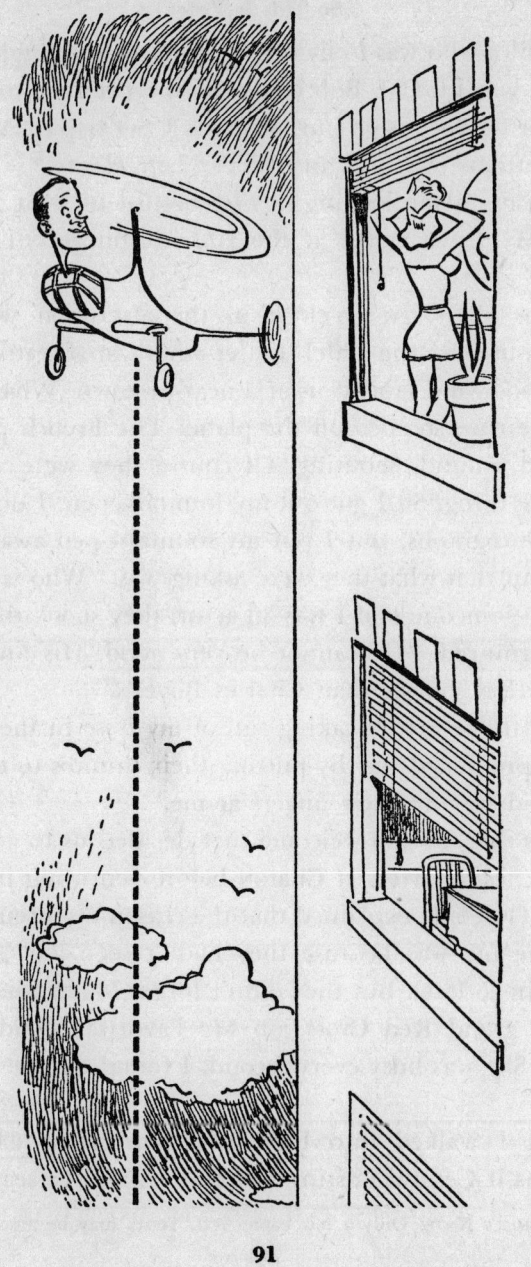

So This Is Peace

at the pilot who was to fly our C-47 across the English Channel. He was Lt. Col. Bob Gates of Aberdeen, South Dakota, the lad who flew us on our very first USO trip to Alaska and the Aleutians way back in *I Never Left Home.**

Bob caught me looking at his chestful of fruit salad and said, "My sister works at the ribbon counter in Marshall Field's."

It was about two o'clock in the afternoon when Bob brought us over the Eiffel Tower—that's an Erector set that made good—and landed us at a near-by town. What a reception when we stepped off the plane! The French people all gathered around, shouting. Of course they were all asking the same thing. So I got out my fountain pen. I don't mind giving autographs. But I put my fountain pen away when I found out that what they were asking was, "Who is this?"

When someone said I was an actor, they shook their heads and murmured, "He cannot be very good. His lower lip is three inches shorter than Charles Boyer's."

Then they started making fun of my nose in their quaint French provincial way by putting their thumbs to their own noses and waving their fingers at me.

It was this rousing welcome that decided us to go directly to USO headquarters at Chatou before venturing into Paris. The USO people explained that the reason the French didn't recognize me was because they hadn't seen any American movies in so long. But they didn't forget Madeleine Carroll. What a grand Red Cross job My Favorite Blonde did in France! She was busy every second, I found out every time I called.

When I walked into USO headquarters at Chatou, it looked as if Central Casting had opened an overseas branch.

---

* PUBLISHER'S NOTE: Only a few copies left. Yours may be among them.

Don't You Know There's a Peace On?

In five minutes I met Alfred Lunt, Lynn Fontanne, and Bozo Snyder. Everyone wore the same uniform, of course, but naturally Lynn Fontanne looked better in hers than Bozo Snyder. And everyone lined up for chow, which, of course, looked better in Bozo Snyder.

There were really so many actors around the place that the breeze from bowing kept the joint air conditioned.

I had luncheon with Reginald Gardiner, Clifton Fadiman, John Kieran, and Franklin P. Adams, the group from "Information, Please!" I couldn't even get my nickel back.

Also on hand were Bea Lillie, entertaining soldiers and trying to forget the son she lost, Billy Van, Constance Dowling, Broadway Harry Rose, Artie Conroy, Cliff Hall, Pat Lane, Harriet Page, Joy Hodges, Charlie Steward, and an old friend, Josephine Del Mar. Josephine had been peddling laughs to the men around the U. K. for twenty-six months. Then she hit the beach at Normandy right after D-Day and had been in France ever since. A big morale booster.

Really, in spite of what you see in your bookstores, a lot of men and women made offshore trips and never said a word about it. So different from You-Know-Who. . . . Guys and gals like Jim Cagney, Gary Cooper, Ann Sheridan, Bill Gargan, who went to the CBI with Paulette Goddard—and who wouldn't.

Even Ed Gardner, the star of that fine radio show, "Duffy's Tavern," the only guy in radio who prides himself on being more illiterate than I am, didn't write a book. And he really had a book to get off his chest after touring the ETO being billed as "Jinx Falkenburg and Company." Jinx also went to the Caribbean, South America, and the CBI Theater with Pat O'Brien. Pat killed 'em with those stories and "Shake Hands with Your Uncle Mike."

So This Is Peace

I guess nobody will ever be able to estimate what a lot of good a steady stream of solid live talent from home did to keep up the spirits of our fighting forces, not only while the going was tough, but after V-E Day when it began to get boring in Europe. And sweating it out for a ticket to Uncle Sugar didn't necessarily mean a little gold eagle in your blue serge lapel.

Actually there were some pretty depressed soldiers around France. A war still raged in the East and many an infantryman who'd come through all the campaigns in the ETO didn't know how much longer his luck might last if it had to be stretched across the islands of the Pacific.

At Chatou we were briefed by the head of the USO in the ETO, Howard Hobbs of Pottsville, Pa., a scholarly-looking six-footer who had two sons in the service. The main thing Hobbs stressed while briefing us for our trip through France and Germany was to go easy on liberating souvenirs. He pleaded with us, "Please, please, don't try to take home any tanks or *Volkswagen.*" I thought that was silly. I don't know how to drive either of them.

But the Army had been having a little trouble. Every time the infantry hit a town that had a building still standing, everyone rushed over and started to paste stamps on it. The father of an Iowa infantry sergeant built a chicken coop and a new barn out of pieces of masonry his son sent home from Germany.

After the briefing, Hobbs showed us a little of the rural countryside around Chatou. A few French peasants courteously tipped their hats to us. I smiled courteously and tipped my hat to a few French girls. But they didn't return the courtesy. Courtesy—that's what you hope to get from a gal when you don't get anything else.

But we weren't interested in rural France. I hadn't been in Paris since 1939, when Chamberlain made his speech warning Americans to get home because his umbrella was starting to leak. I left Paris so fast I forgot to pay my hotel bill. When I went back to get my trunk I found some sneaking Nazi had made it a member of the Third Reich. But I've lost so much luggage!

That's why I wasn't impressed with the news of postwar, airtight luggage. What's new about luggage that air can't get into? For years I've had luggage even *I* couldn't get into.

But when they apply this airtight-luggage idea to pocketbooks, guess whose moths will smother to death.

Aside from my luggage, things in Paris hadn't changed much. They looked wonderful. Only most of them were just dating American *soldiers*. However, I really didn't have time for that sort of thing—I kept telling myself.

Really, my last trip to France impressed me so much that when I came home I made a picture called *Monsieur Beaucaire*. This impressed the French so much I hear I can't go back to France. They might even bar Laurence Olivier for his streamlined version of William Shakespeare's *Henry the Fifth*. In the original title it was called *Henry the Fift*. That's the first inkling anyone ever got that Shakespeare came from Brooklyn. And it came as quite a blow to Noel Coward.

Olivier really didn't make the French look too good either before, during, or after the Battle of Agincourt. Incidentally, the scenes of that battle fascinated a lot of ex-GI's because it showed the origin of the LST, the tank trap and the tank, as well as an early demonstration of the fact that a fast, light, smart, mobile force can lick sheer blundering power. Besides showing a lot of guys who already knew this that it was true as far back as the seventeenth century, it also made us very intimately acquainted with Shakespeare. After seeing the picture *Henry the Fifth* we were all ready to call the Bard Shakesie or Bill. And we were convinced that Hank the Five or, as some called him, H the Vee, was a right nice gee.

Instead of being art, the picture turned out to be the greatest piece of British propaganda to hit America since we were given permission to eat roast beef without Yorkshire pudding. We liked, for instance, the way the English pronounced all the French names as they're spelled instead of the way some Parisian with asthma and a bad sinus attack might be forced to say them. I wish I'd thought of some of those pronunciations when I was in Paris. People might not have understood what I was talking about, but at least I'd have known.

We were in Paris mainly to do a three-way broadcast called "Atlantic Spotlight" in which Ben Grauer in New York, Leslie Mitchell in London, and I in Paris tossed dialogue across one ocean, two continents, and three networks. We tried to get Orson Welles to join us, but at that time they hadn't tried radar to Mars. I say "at that time" because this book won't be published until the winter of 1946. By that time I figure they'll have tried everything, and the midnight rocket to Mars will leave three nights a week from the Cahuenga Blvd. Greyhound Bus Terminal.

Don't You Know There's a Peace On?

The quickest way to get around Paris, I knew, was by subway. But in Paris they call the subway the Métro. So I walked. I'm from Paramount. Transportation was very scarce. You could walk into a room, drunk, with your shirttail hanging out, insult your host's wife, and spit tobacco juice on the oriental rug ... but if you said, "I've got a car outside," you had more pals than Dale Carnegie.

And while dodging taxis around the Arc de Triomphe I ran into two of the Army of the United States' most celebrated corporals, Mickey Rooney and Bobby Breen. Rather Bobby Breen ran into me. He was in one of the taxis. He got out and said, "Remember me?"

I said, "Why, sure. You're Bobby Breen. I remember you when you weren't much bigger than one of Eddie Cantor's eyeballs."

Mickey Rooney was standing in a jeep, screaming excitedly at the natives. Of course, he has to stand up in a jeep. It's the only way he can see over the side. But Mickey had a right to be excited. He'd just heard he'd become the father of a seven-pound baby boy. It was hard for me to imagine Andy Hardy having an Andy Hardy. But listening to what his fellow GI's said about Rooney made it easy to understand why the little "big man" of MGM was considered one of the biggest little men in the AUS.

There's an old saying that if you sit at a sidewalk table at the Café de la Paix in Paris everybody you know will go by. I just walked along the Paris streets and pretty soon the Café de la Paix went by. I ran into Walter O'Keefe's brother, Jack, who was writing a very funny column for the 1st Division newspaper, *The Traveler*. And Shep Fields was there with his all-woodwind band. But I hear Shep made out all right with his Rippling Rhythm. He sold his surplus bubbles

So This Is Peace

to Margie Hart. Almost the only guy I didn't meet in Paris was Red Skelton. I suppose he was following me, as usual.

At one show we did, after a broadcast at the Paris Olympia theater, they had a French master of ceremonies who introduced me as Bobe Hape. I didn't know his name but I felt like getting even by introducing Maurice Chevalier as Morris Sheval. But I didn't have the heart. Chevalier was really great. He gave a show dressed in a white turtleneck sweater and bright red pants. Of course he sang "Louise." The boys gave him a fine hand and Maurice said, "Eet touches my 'eart to theenk that you all ware jus' leetle boys when I was makeeng pictaires in the United States and that you all still remembaire me." He looked older and lacked his straw skimmer, but he still had plenty of that lower-lip charm.

One of the gala things about Paris right after liberation was the fact that the French Army would hold a Grand Dress Parade at the drop of an anniversary. In fact, every day the gendarmes roped off ten blocks on either side of the Arc de Triomphe just in case. Every time de Gaulle wanted a cup of coffee, the French Army sent out two regiments. Later in the morning a small cadre went down for a second cup.

And speaking of de Gaulle, he was not only in Paris at the same time I was, he was in New York when I got there, and he was in Chicago when I arrived there on my way back to Hollywood. He must have a nice collection of towels, too. I wouldn't have known he was in Chicago and stopping at my hotel, but he had the room under mine and his head bumping against the ceiling kept me awake for three hours.

We lived in pretty good style in Paris. We couldn't get billets at any of the military hotels because they were all filled with congressmen. There were so many congressmen in town they began investigating each other. So we were given

Don't You Know There's a Peace On?

some space at the Hôtel Claridge.

When we'd been there about fifteen minutes we found out that to get anything done you had to figure more angles than a freshman geometry student. You have to pretend you know only the best people. For instance, I had to have a suit pressed to do the broadcast at the Olympia theater. I wasn't being dudish about it. Even Crosby would have admitted the suit needed pressing. Ruth Denas picked it up and played two choruses of "Tico Tico" on it before she discovered it wasn't her accordion.

So I rang for a bellboy and when I told him I needed the suit back in an hour he just laughed at me. Then he looked at the suit and laughed at *it*. I tried to explain in my broken French how important it was, but the guy was listening in broken English and couldn't understand me. Finally I said I had to have cocktails with de Gaulle. *Voilà!* In ten minutes he had the suit back with a razor-edge press. In fact, it was such a razor edge that after reconversion, the left leg of my pants was what Gregory Peck had in his hand behind Bergman's back in those ads for *Spellbound*.

Traveling around Paris by jeep, we naturally picked up all service people who asked for a lift. If we saw any WAC's we asked them if they'd let us give them a lift. That's how we got to meet WAC Corporal Mary Korval of the Paris Military Switchboard (she'd just improved her rating by marrying a sergeant) and WAC PFC Mickie Kumpe. We took them to Rainbow Corner, the famous Paris Red Cross Canteen. PFC Kumpe had spent twenty-four months overseas out of twenty-six months in the Army. She was postmaster—not postmistress—of Little Rock, Ark., and I'll bet she did a great business for Uncle Sam. Mickie is the type it's fun to play post office with. You can imagine, after two years in the ETO, how anxious the service gals were to get home and out of uniform.

I didn't realize how much demobilization meant to the gals until we played San Diego Naval Training Station one Tuesday after V-J Day, three years after we had first played there. At that time the war was going so badly in the Pacific that when Skinnay Ennis and his band arrived from Hollywood in a Navy bus a chief petty officer jumped aboard and hollered, "Quiet, you guys! You're in the Navy now!" The musicians all immediately started reaching for Petrillo's phone number. They were just about to shave Skin's head and shove him into tight pants when I sprung him. The CPO said, "I was worried. If they're taking men like this

Don't You Know There's a Peace On?

guy things must be so tough none of us has much chance of coming out alive."

It kind of gave me a funny feeling to look back on those black days when servicemen really felt that way and then look out at the bunch of Waves whose coming-out party we'd come down to the base to help celebrate. Three thousand Waves were being "pointed" out of the Navy.

A Wave, as I've explained many times, is an old salt in a new shaker, who goes down to the sea in slips.

Every one of those gals had enlisted to release a man for active duty, and every one of them wanted to get out of the Navy and start looking for him. I wouldn't say they were all thinking about getting married, but I dropped a nickel in a pay phone near the Wave barracks and the gong played Mendelssohn's "Wedding March."

There was a story going around that a civilian stopped in front of the gate to tie his shoe and by the time he got up off his knee, he was married, had spent two weeks at Niagara Falls, and had made the first three payments on a honeymoon cottage.

A gal in the WAC told me that most of the girls had been in service so long they were really tired of taking orders. They wanted to get married and start dishing it out. The only use they had for the word "obey" was if it had "love, honor, and" in front of it.

And, of course, they were interested in getting back into civilian clothes. One San Diego dress shop had to have the porter spend the first two hours every morning scraping lipstick off the show windows. The WAC's weren't particularly interested in stuff by Adrian or Schiaparelli. Any one of them would have been willing to climb into something by Pillsbury, had they been able to find a flour bag that fit.

So This Is Peace

But they had to be careful about clothes. I heard about one Wave who got out, bought herself a pair of high-heeled shoes, and blacked out from the altitude. Women are really strange. They talk about fancy clothes. Yet most of those Waves, when they got discharged, actually went right out to buy themselves slacks. I can't figure out women. But I love playing around with the combination.

There were a couple of odd cases among the Waves being

discharged. One ex-yeoman went back to her job as secretary, but she'd become so indoctrinated by the Navy that her boss had to sew three gold stripes on his sleeve before she'd sit on his lap. Another gal, trying for her discharge, paid some phony guy fifty bucks to act as her husband. But they found out about it and threw her into the brig. So I gave her back her money. It seemed like the only right thing to do.

But not one of those Waves was any more anxious to get a Lame Duck sewed above her heart than were the GI's around Paris. The City of Light had nothing to offer most of them that they wouldn't trade for the Malt Shop on the corner where the people and the jukebox spoke their language. Yes, sir, they just couldn't wait to get their discharges and say "Au revoir" to their officers. "Au revoir," that's Parisian for "Pardon my combat boot!"

From Paris we ducked over to Amiens to cross sneers with the men of the 438th Troop Carrier Group, the boys who went

So This Is Peace

in first at Normandy, spearheading the airborne infantry and paratroopers. I couldn't write about all these names of outfits and places during the war. In those days the censors were so careful about security that every time I laid an egg, a second lieutenant ran out and candled it.

CHAPTER 6

Worn World

NINETEEN HUNDRED AND FORTY-FIVE, in war and peace, was the year Bing Crosby stayed off the air. And everybody who wanted him to come and hustle their stuff—and that was almost everybody—started waving offers in front of Happy Hips' tired old peepers. Literally, Senior had them offering him cheese factories, oil wells, and any money he cared to name to return to the networks. And one of the networks even offered him the network. Bing didn't accept, but even so, by the spring of 1946, he had every sponsor in radio and a few eager-beaver entries crooning for *him*.

Ford was one of the few companies that didn't even try to get Bing Crosby. They hired his younger brother, Bob, on the theory that a new and younger generation was growing up and getting ready to "watch the Crosbys go by."

Finally, one enterprising agency figured out a way Bing could broadcast without getting on his feet, and Bing signed quicker than Everett could say, "How about my ten per cent?" He is going to work for Philco, a radio which for years advertised no squint, no squat, no stoop, and now has done a sharp about-face and hired all three of them at $30,000 a week. Bing is going to cut records which will be played nationally in the biggest wax deal since Fibber McGee had Edward Arnold and Sydney Greenstreet wrestle on his program. The thought of having a recorded program coast to coast has greatly disturbed some of the other networks. One major skein president was so despondent he walked into the censor's office and committed hara-kiri by hurling himself on a pointed innuendo. A more enterprising network, sensing a trend, attempted to steal a march in the recorded field by hiring a comedian with a nose like a needle, but I'd been spoken for. On the surface, of course, this step may not be world shaking, but as the Warner Brothers said when they offered Henry Luce some commissary hash, "There'll Be Some Changes Made."

Of course you can't blame Bing or anyone else for holding out for as much of anything as he can get. A man with a family the size of his needs plenty of that government skin to keep meat and potatoes on the table. Back in May, 1946, I walked into a restaurant in San Francisco, picked up a menu, and saw "Broiled Halibut ... $7.50." I knew the price of living was going up, but that was more inflation than we had even in Hollywood; so I called the maître d', pointed to the price of halibut, and said, "How about this?"

He shrugged his shoulders and answered, "What can we do? Since Greer Garson fell in the ocean, you can't even look at a flounder."

This was right after Metro-Goldwyn-Mayer started advertising, "Gable's Back and Garson's Got Him." Maybe it was Clark, struggling to get away, that made Greer lose her balance and fall into Carmel Bay. I'm told the people up around the Monterey Peninsula got so much publicity out of her dip that they're thinking of changing the name of historic and beautiful Point Lobos to Garson's Plunge.

But that "Gable's Back and Garson's Got Him" routine was really started by me. Right after V-J Day I returned to Hollywood and sent Paramount a wire saying that, like Lassie, I'd come home. They immediately took trade-paper ads announcing, "Hope Is Back and Who Wants Him?"

Paramount, that's where I've come closer to having my breathing cut off than in any of the military theaters of operation I've ever visited. People used to claim that anyone who left Paramount to enlist in the Commandos was a coward. Why do you think they call us Para. Troupers?

Just to give you an idea what kind of risk we are for the insurance people, when old Father Time and I were working on *The Road to Utopia,* we did a scene where we had to lie on the floor in front of a big roaring fire and pretend to be asleep, while a big roaring bear came in the door and pretended we weren't tasty. He was supposed to sniff us and go away. I must have had the script of the picture in my pocket, because when the bear sniffed *me* he started to growl. My goose pimples were so big it looked as if I had twenty-seven heads. And that was just the rehearsal. I said to the trainer, "What happens if this bear isn't a member of my union?"

"Don't worry," the trainer assured me, "he's a member of Equity and the Screen Actors' Guild."

The next day the bear nearly clawed off the trainer's arm. Maybe the trainer's union was AF of L and the bear's, CIO. But can you imagine Crosby, who won the Academy Award, lying on the floor, getting sniffed by a bear? That was right after he'd sung "Toora Loora Loora" and had Barry Fitzgerald sniffing.

So This Is Peace

And, as if winning an Oscar weren't enough, what does Lucky Lard do but turn around and get himself in a picture with Ingrid Bergman! That's like voting yourself the Pulitzer Prize *and* the Nobel Award all on the same ballot.

But before we go on to less important matters, every GI I'd ever met who happened to be in one of the several theaters of operation visited by Miss Bergman spoke of her as if he were saying his prayers. It's no wonder her name in front of a theater is practically the same as hanging out a sign saying "Standing Room Only." Of course the way things are now, they don't even have to give dishes with *my* pictures.

Peace has been a big boon to all kinds of entertainment.

Worn World

Movies, the drama, concerts, ballet . . . they're all sell-outs. Some authorities think this is because everyone is starved for diversion. My theory is that the housing shortage has created a floating population that will go anywhere they think there's a chance to sit down for a little while. I know a man who runs an all-night movie house on Hollywood Boulevard who's thinking of increasing the admission and including a club breakfast.

That's what I like about show business. There's always someone in there trying. Just to show you how far show business will go, the first two people I met when I landed on Guadalcanal were Hollywood agents. One was Sergeant Red Hirshon of the Army, who used to be with the William Morris office, and the other was Captain Walter Johnson of the Marines, who was with MCA. Those two outfits *would* be covering the territory.

I understand the United Nations has a plan drawn up under which William Morris gives all its band clients back to Music Corporation of America and MCA gives all its actors back to William Morris. Of course they won't be able to act on that until Byrnes learns to drink vodka. When I spoke to Hirshon about the two agents on the island and asked him if he was there looking over the natives, to line up extra talent for Central Casting, he said, "Every time an actor captures ten Japs he has to send one to the Morris office." Those guys will never give up their ten per cent.

Besides the agents, on Guadal., we ran into Zerubica, who carried the ball for UCLA. He skippered a PT boat. Bell, the All-American from Purdue, was in the same line of work. Roxy Rothafel, Jr., was doing a little camping out with the United States Marine Corps. People, people, people! There

So This Is Peace

were an awful lot of them we all knew on Pacific duty. We even had friends among the enemy.

What I mean is best explained in a letter Bud Crooks wrote to his friend Abe Grudd, of Yermo, California. Abe sent me the letter, saying:

"Am certain you will be more than interested in contents of a letter we got from one of the Mojave Desert Gang down in the Netherlands East Indies. Bud Crooks writes:

" 'Bob Hope was here some time ago. He sure had plenty of fellows to see the show. Everyone within traveling distance came to see the performance. The payoff came a few days ago when some Japs were taken prisoner. They said they had enjoyed Bob's show. No more picture shows for me. You never can tell who might be sitting next to you.' "

On Guadal. we thought they were kidding when they told us that Japs used to sneak in at night and catch our shows from the trees. They were probably the ones who started the rumor around Japan that we were using poison gas. It's a funny feeling to think of the enemy watching your show through telescope sights. That means a guy peeks at you through a telescope on a gun barrel, pulls the trigger, and you're a sight!

Yes, our second trip to Europe was more pleasant. Because no one was shooting at anyone. We just rode in bucket seats from place to place and hoped the plane would keep aloft so that we wouldn't turn out to be just a drop in the bucket.

Really, we were all hardly able to wait till we could get out of Paris and have a look at Germany. So, even though the weather wasn't the best, we left Le Bourget on the first plane the Army would let us ride.

While waiting for the weather to lift a little, we were entertained by Colonel Luke Powell and the officers of the 438th. Entertained, that means we told them our jokes and they gave us France's wine. Then we took off in a C-47. The haze was so thick the pigeons were digging tunnels, but I wasn't a bit worried. I slept. That Ovaltine's wonderful.

For lunch, two of the guys aboard—Staff Sergeants Papadikas of Salt Lake City and Ernest Parket of South Carolina—broke out a box of what was then the new Ten-in-One rations. It was designed to feed ten men for one day. Or one man can eat it in ten minutes. All I know is that my civilian friends in London considered it a big treat, and the guys really liked it a lot better than the old C and K ration, and here's why. It contained little cans of cheese, bacon, butter, cereal, delicious ground meat, fruit cake, preserves, crackers, candy, cigarettes, water-purifying tablets, and toilet paper. When I saw that I sat right down and started this book.

With all that food, I was sorry I hadn't brought along Edward Arnold's stomach. Our boys really had the stuff to eat in those days and I've got the girdle to prove it.

I kept looking till I found one. Some people gave up hunting for stuff that was hard to get because they found out that the stove manufacturers designed a lot of new stoves but held them back till the food came in. The food packers packed plenty of provisions but held them back till the new refrigerators came in. The home builders designed a lot of new houses but held them back till the appliances came in. So when the people came in to buy any of the new stuff, they found it was all being held back till the Republicans came in.

After six years of being unable to resupply their kitchens, housewives suddenly found they didn't have a pot to cook in. Luckily, this didn't bother them for long. Because there was

So This Is Peace

nothing to cook. This same shortage suddenly struck all the new restaurants, which began to disappear as fast as they'd opened. First, meat disappeared. Then butter disappeared. Then bread disappeared. Then the manager disappeared because he couldn't stand hearing people telling him that their portion had disappeared under the gravy. But the disappearance that finally forced us to stay home was when the prices disappeared, through the ceiling.

It was a tough rap and we couldn't even take to drink because the liquor had also disappeared. The country was really dis-spirited, in spite of the fact that the counters of the liquor stores looked like rum row. Besides rum, all liquor dealers had to offer was a Scotch-type Blended Energine and a six-month-old liqueur-type 100-proof Carbona, either of which was guaranteed to take care of the spots before your eyes. White mule was even cut so they had to label it straight burro.

The dealers' shelves were filled with European cordials and vermouths made in the Argentine, real Russian vodka from Mexico, Mexican tequila imported by the Hudson Bay Company (Paul Muni, Pres.), and genuine Rhine wine from Chile.

Of course there were plenty of domestic whines, too, from customers looking for Straight Kentucky Bourbon and being offered Fine Napa Valley Neufchâtel.

The grain shortage really hit the staggering distillers right where they were bonded and made the beer-brewing industry into an ailing one. The heavy-drinking South began to experiment with a potable cotton gin, and night-club drinks got weaker than the floor shows, which naturally caused a falling off in business. Hundreds of hard-working cigarette girls, cloakroom attendants, and show girls had to get dressed and go home.

And the liquor that was served straight across the bars showed up in ponies with bottoms so thick they were exactly flush with the lip. All you could leave within the cup was a kiss. It got so that the Army couldn't even supply its officers' clubs. But during the war they got it to take care of their men in rest centers. I know. Because as we flew toward Bremen, Crew Chief Elder F. Loney of Columbus, Ohio, took the bucket seat next to mine and said, "These C-47's are certainly hauling some strange cargo since the war ended."

I didn't get it. He sat down, took one look at me, and started talking about strange cargo.

"The other day we came to Nice," he continued, "with a load of whisky and fourteen hundred beer glasses for a bar the Army's opening. Things sure change. When I was stateside, the Army was trying to close the bars. Here they're opening them."

"Have any trouble with that cargo of whisky and beer glasses?" I asked.

"Nope," said Loney. "With a load like that anything flies."

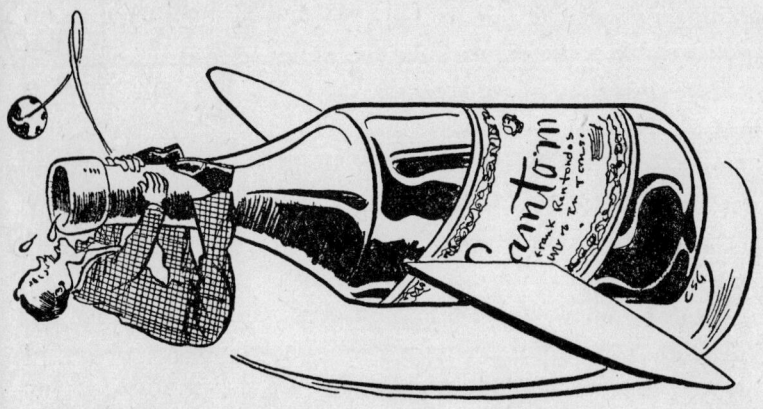

If they'd been forced down they could have put up a saloon and gone into business.

We were really lucky on our trip to Germany to have as our CO Major Mike Cullen, the Traveler's Aid of the ETO. Mike's only family is his mother in Columbus, Ohio, and instead of her writing fan letters to the stars, they write to her about what a wonderful job Mike did taking care of them on their European trips.

Mike started being the Cook's Man of the USO back in 1943, when he chaperoned Frances Langford, Jerry Colonna, Tony Romano, Jack Pepper, and me all over Africa and Sicily. (As set down in all its graphic detail in the first volume of This Roving Boy's Series, *I Never Left Home.**)

Flying toward Bremen, Mike told me all about the chain of movie theaters he was running for the Army, two hundred

---
* PUBLISHER'S NOTE: Only 75,000 copies left. Mail your order today.

houses in the ETO, all showing the latest films. Of course this operation has been greatly curtailed. But we still have plenty of men in Europe and should continue to have, and we've got to keep feeding them the kind of entertainment they need and understand: American pictures, radio shows, and, of course, live talent. They tell me the main job of an occupational force is just to be there and be seen. It's the job of show business to see that the force also has something to look at. Talking about his management problems, Mike said, "One thing I *don't* have to worry about is refunds."

"When there's no admission charge, I don't suppose you get many squawks about the quality of the pictures from your customers."

"Only when we show one of your pictures," Mike said.

Before I could make some stinging rejoinder (Note to printer: That's a *g*), Mike pointed out the window at the ground.

"It's Wesel," he said, "where the 17th Airborne and Paratroopers landed during our first crossing of the Rhine. You can still see the gliders parked around town."

It really looked messed up. The reason the gliders were parked around town was because that's about all there was left of Wesel—parking space.

There didn't seem to be a roof left in the whole city. But they really didn't need roofs. There weren't any walls, either.

Looking down at this ruin with me was Annabelle Mattox of Florence, Alabama. Miss Mattox was Civ Sec to Com of OSS in ETO. That's the Army's answer to *Variety* headlines. Boiled down to a few hundred words, it means she was a civilian working for the Office of Strategic Services. That's the Army's FBI and it's so secret Miss Mattox wouldn't even talk to me. Or maybe that approach Crosby gave me is getting a little stale. Maybe there aren't any more girls who go for a guy when he snaps his suspenders, spits through his teeth, and says, "Butter me up, kiddo, I'm the toast of the town."

But I didn't have time to worry about a girl. That proves how excited I was to land at Bremen and set foot on German soil. We were in England in 1943, doing shows at the different bomber bases, and we'd see the men and planes coming back from working over Germany. I could hardly wait to see what they'd done.

So it was a tremendous wallop to step out of our C-47 at Bremen airport. The band from the all-Negro 399th that was to be with our show was lined up and playing "Thanks for the Memory," on key. I had a record made of it to prove to Skinnay Ennis that it *can* be done.

Then we entered Bremen and got the first closeup of what a job our Air Force and the RAF had done. The Germans started the war because they wanted living room. Well, they've got plenty of room now—it's where the buildings used to be. It was really wonderful to look at bomb damage you could feel good about. Actually, Bremen hadn't had it too hard. The dock area was badly smashed, but at that time the people looked pretty healthy. Better than they did in France. They seemed well fed and well dressed. Lots of the women were wearing silk stockings, while American and English girls still had to smile in lisle.

We did our first show in Germany at seven o'clock that evening in the General Ike Stadium, a race track and athletic field on the edge of Bremen. Our audience was 8000 guys from the 29th Division, all combat men and ninety per cent wore the Purple Heart. They were pretty cocky and had a right to be. What an outfit!

I had played for them in England in 1943, when they were training for the invasion. But there weren't many left who could remember that.

These guys had landed at Normandy at a cost of about 21,000 men, fought their way up through northern France, at Aachen, Saint-Lô, in the Bulge, and across Germany. They were a great audience. Their motto was "Let's Go!" And they kept hollering it all during my show.

It was in Bremen that we began to get used to a new kind of audience. The last time we'd played the ETO the men who'd seen our shows had been all hopped up with anticipation of impending combat and they wanted to like everything. But in 1945 they listened to our routines while packing.

Literally, every place we went to we got the same farewell when the show was over and we were trying to sneak out of town. It wasn't "Good-by" and it wasn't "See you again!" To a man, the guys hollered, "Take us with you!"

The same men who'd fought so hard to get into Germany were fighting just as hard to get out. This, in spite of the fact that the Army had over two million liters of beer they were giving away free. A liter, that's a king-size quart.

But when most of the guys came home, it wasn't long before they began to miss those great big liters. They would have made nice places to live in. I honestly didn't realize how serious the housing situation was until the day I walked up to a phone booth and saw a guy in it depositing a hatful of nickels. I said to him, "Brother, you must be calling China."

He said, "No. I'm just paying my rent."

I heard of one veteran who didn't have any trouble finding a place to live. His experience just shows you, you have to be practical. After looking for an apartment for a few days, he decided to face facts. So he nailed his medals together, had a roof put on, and moved in. He papered the walls with his campaign ribbons.

Of course just any place won't do for a lot of these men. They have very definite ideas of what they want and really need to be comfortable. And they certainly deserve to be comfortable after what they went through. So until they find what suits them perfectly, they keep searching. A kid who lives near me in North Hollywood, who was a ball turret gunner for three years, couldn't find what he wanted until someone was kind enough to rent him his goldfish bowl.

The veterans, naturally, aren't taking this situation without a fight. They know that things are bad. But they also know that when things are bad, they'll get worse unless you do something about them. The best thing to do is go right to the top. One discharged sailor walked all the way from

So This Is Peace

Los Angeles to Sacramento to see Governor Warren about a place to live. The Governor was very helpful and sympathetic. He said, "I'll do everything I can for you . . . just step into my tent."

The housing shortage has honestly caused everybody to be sympathetic. But the veterans are all agreed that if you believe anyone's going to be very helpful you're a pathetic simp.

Actually, I guess Hollywood is really trying to do something about the housing shortage. There's the Rodger Young Village of Quonset Huts, and, besides that, Hollywood is the only place where people who live in trees have a "share-the-limb" plan.

Although, when we played Tacoma, Marine Sergeant Jimmy Sames showed us thirty or forty brand-new homes, all beautifully painted green to match the lumber they were made of. Jimmy admitted the lumber he put into his houses was green. But he said he played fair with the people. He gave them each a brand-new set of pruning shears.

One GI said he was tickled to death that his three-room bungalow was built of green lumber. In one year it grew into a ten-room boardinghouse and bore four prefabricated garages at harvesttime.

Of course those prefabricated houses are really sensational. After our show in Pittsburgh a colonel I hadn't seen since we shared an air-raid shelter in Algiers came backstage and told me if I wanted to buy any ready-built homes, he'd be glad to ship me as many as my relatives needed and give me a rate. What a country!

Today you can actually phone someone to send over a house, go to a double-feature movie, and when you come back you find your prefabricated home all ready with a prefabricated dinner waiting. All you have to do is add boiling water, let cook for ten minutes . . . and then go out to eat.

But the prefabricated houses are really cute. I saw a lot of different kinds. They come in several styles. Some even look like houses. They can be put up in anywhere from two to ten hours by three strong men and brought down in anywhere from five to ten seconds by one strong wind. Somewhere along our route I saw an ad for a prefab house that said, "Anyone who can change a tire can put up this house." That didn't sound like a house. It sounded more like a flat.

But if prefabs are the answer to how to scrap the NO-VACANCY signs, I'm for them. I sleep so much better indoors.

And the situation is so bad it's beginning to affect the farms. People are going farther and farther to find a place to live. Last Halloween most of the smart farmers hid out in the back with their shotguns. They weren't so much afraid some kid would overturn the little house; they were afraid some family might move in.

I even saw a turtle with a head sticking out the side of his shell. He was subletting part of the shell to a family of field mice.

So This Is Peace

But the situation really isn't funny. With a shortage of building materials, a shortage of people willing to build small, inexpensive homes, and a shortage of memory on the part of all of us who once said, "Nothing will be too good for the boys when they come back," our vets are finding the housing situation pretty rugged. And the worst rap of all is when an ex-EM with his wife and baby finally finds a vacancy and can't take it because the landlord won't allow children. The only trouble with children is that some of them grow to be that kind of landlord.

And I know what to do with them. Send them to Christmas Island.

CHAPTER 7

South Sea Island Makeshift

CHRISTMAS ISLAND made a great impression on me. The only industry of the island is the manufacture of fertilizer. The birds run the business. I got a nice welcome.

We arrived on Christmas Island in July, 1944, in a big Liberator named *7th Heaven*. The plane had an icebox and reclining chairs. Christmas Island had nothing, except, of course, those birds and their fertilizer business. But this didn't surprise me.

Over the Pacific, on the way in, Captain Orme described Christmas to us by saying, "It's a guano island inhabited by thousands of goony birds."

I said, "That's a fine way to talk about the Navy." I have an uncle who was in the Navy, so I'm touchy. They say he was a swivel-chair admiral. But he earned a lot of medals. And if he ever stands up they're going to pin them where he earned them.

"No, really," Orme insisted, "that's what live there. Goony

So This Is Peace

birds. I understand that before the war England and the United States had quite a diplomatic tussle as to who owned the atoll."

"Valuable, huh?"

"Judge for yourself," Frank said. "England claimed it was ours and we claimed it was theirs. Now we're fighting to give it back to the Japs." He then went back to his flying.

What he didn't tell us was that Christmas is the largest atoll in the world. Also the dullest. Besides the goony birds, the only entertainment the men stationed there had until we arrived was the Gary Cooper troupe that had played the island over a year before. So naturally, after we did our show, everyone gathered around and begged us to see if we could get Coop to come back. He made a great impression all through the Pacific area. There are stories of how he'd walk through the jungle and pick Jap snipers out of the tops of coconut palms. Coop says this isn't true. That maybe he did pick an occasional sniper, but all he was after was coconuts. He's such a modest guy.

They assigned one soldier as our guide while we were on Christmas. You needed a guide about as much as you need a guide in the rumble seat of a cut-down jalopy. But Sammy— that's all I ever heard anyone call him—did his best. The first thing he showed us was the distillery. Colonna was pulling back his strainer and getting ready to sample some of the local spirits when Sammy said, "They distill about 5000 gallons of water a day here."

"Egad!" shrieked Colonna. "What a disgusting disappointment!"

"Only trouble is," Sammy went on, "5000 gallons of water ain't enough. They use it only for drinking and cooking. For washing, shaving, and bathing we gotta use salt water. I been

South Sea Island Makeshift

in salt water so much that when my eyes get bloodshot I look like a stuffed olive with a double pimento."

Among other pleasant features of lovely Christmas Island were the flying cockroaches, blister bugs, and land crabs. Sounds like a description of a lot of our friends, doesn't it? But those land crabs are something. They move sideways like Bing's horses. And the blister bugs can't be pushed around. They're hard to get rid of. They have to be given the brush very carefully, like a gossip columnist. If you try to get rough with them and swat them, they give off an acid that burns you. It's quite a sight, though, doing a show for a lot of guys all sitting around giving bugs the brush. But we were grateful. If the bugs hadn't been there, we might have gotten it.

Yes, sir, after twenty-four hours on Christmas in July, we began to see how easy it was for some of the guys to get so lonely they went a little pineapple and had to be sent home for some psychiatric treatment. And even more guys might have found Christmas too tough to take if it hadn't been for Major Buck Rogers and Captain Francis (Packy) Hughes of the ATC. These two men made it their business to see that stuff like ice cream and other luxuries got shipped to spots like Christmas Island on holidays. Two guys like Buck and Packy can build a lot of morale for an army. And at spots like Christmas it sure was needed. During our show, while Frances was singing, "You Made Me Love You," I noticed a young officer looking at a picture of his wife and baby and crying quietly.

Sure, they had things to do sometimes; a little work . . . and they'd made themselves a golf course. They used land crabs for caddies.

I'll never forget that golf course. The fairways were so

hard you could drive a ball 400 yards. The only trouble was the holes were only 300. The only way you could tell you were on a green was that the sand was packed down a little tighter. But it was easy to tell where you teed off. That was where you took another salt tablet. The only way you could tee off was to find a nice unneurotic goony bird and hit fast.

It was a fine course, but there was absolutely nothing new to relieve the monotony and that's what makes a man rock-happy. One guy told me some of the kids got so lonely they started talking to the goony birds.

"That's bad," I said.

"No, that's not so bad," he told me. "It's not really serious until the goonies start talking back. Then you know you've missed too many boats. The biggest excitement we ever had here was when the Army sent in twenty-two cows."

"Cows?"

"Bob," he said slowly, and a mist came over his eyes, "when those twenty-two big containers of fresh milk walked down the gangplank, I wanted to cry. Some of the guys applauded like those Elsies were a line of Rita Hayworths."

Besides the few jokes we tossed around we played a fast five innings of baseball with the men. Naturally, the goonies umpired. And we had quite a team. I played the hot corner, Barney Dean was short (four feet eleven), Colonna was on second and Romano on the guitar. The two girls played the field and vice versa. Baseball really is my game. I'm always playing infield. When we did our show for the Seattle civilians in Sick's Stadium, they knew this and put the stage on second base. The nearest seats were about seventy-five yards away. It was too bad that was before Mike Jacobs started the fad of charging $100 for that kind of seat. But I was glad we were on second base in Seattle. In most places I didn't get to first base.

Whenever I tell people I play baseball they laugh the way they used to laugh when that guy sat down to play the piano. This is silly. I played for East High in Cleveland and stayed in that fast competition until I joined the Hoffman Ice Cream Club and got frozen out. I used to be a spitball pitcher. In fact, I still drool a little.

So you see it was perfectly natural for me to buy a piece of the Cleveland Indians. Of course, it wasn't just my interest in baseball that prompted this investment. I like to have

So This Is Peace

a place to stay when I go home to Cleveland (my relatives are always crowded with their relatives) and living conditions are so tough I had to give the Indians some money to get a wigwam.

There were other reasons, too. I've always loved going to baseball games. It's the only chance I get to yell at a fellow with muscles. And I felt I was getting a little too old to climb the fence any more to see the games at League Park. I wanted to find out what it was like to walk in the main gate. Of course, I only have a one-sixth interest in the team, which means I'm allowed to manage it for three innings during a double-header.

I know I got into the right organization because all the sports writers agreed that what the Indians needed most was hope. Naturally, Bing volunteered to help, too. So the board of directors met and took a vote and we decided we could use him at second . . . as the bag. Now it wouldn't surprise me if Bing bought the League and sold Cleveland.

Copycat Crosby quickly followed this purchase by one of his own, a quarter interest in the Pittsburgh Pirates. Bing should be right at home there. I won't say that he's a pirate exactly, but every time it's pay day at Paramount he shows up with a black patch over his eye. Pittsburgh used to be world famous as the city with the Golden Triangle. Well, if I know Crosby they better watch it or someday they'll wake up and find their hypotenuse is missing. One of the more jealous actors insisted Bing bought the club to insure infield positions for his four boys, but when I taunted him with this fact he denied it. Already Bing's influence is being reflected in the club. Whenever young Andy Lardy sits down on the bench four relief pitchers and the water boy have to move to the ground.

South Sea Island Makeshift

As for me, getting a chance to join the Indians was just a matter of "when a friend needs a Feller." I was so proud of buying into a ball team, I sent my English relatives copies of American sports pages. It worked out fine. They've stopped writing me for money to come to "the new world." They're now scared to come here. Headlines like "Indians Scalp Yankees" and "Braves Beat Giants" did it. About the only headline that didn't frighten them was "Cardinals Clean Up Reds." But I'm happy.

When they ask me what my position with the team is, I say bat boy. Naturally, I have another boy to help lift the heavier bats. But I sure hope the team does well. If it doesn't I may join the Mexican League. I have my reasons for wanting to see Cleveland in the World Series. It's not so much the principle of the thing. It's the money. As somebody once said, "In the world of sports . . . when the game is over and the final score is up . . . it's not so much how well you played . . . but did you win?"

Mainly because I live in California the Cleveland Club has asked me to keep my eye peeled south of the border so we don't lose any players to the Mexican League. And without their asking I'm keeping my eyes on the cashier in that respect, too. But the Mexican League *does* have such inducements—those gay señoritas, particularly. I tried to fool the boys back in Cleveland by getting Jerry Colonna to walk through the infield in a mantilla, but his mustache was too big.

If the Indians don't do well enough under the new ownership, the people of Cleveland may send us to some spot like Christmas Island, and if it gets too crowded there, they could send the overflow to Canton Island.

There's another little beauty spot in the South Pacific.

So This Is Peace

The only difference between Christmas and Canton was that Canton had fresh water. And it's so hard, a *duck* would roll off *it*. But when you take a shower on Christmas, you wind up with a handful of salt.

Canton isn't as big as Christmas. In fact, it's so small that the ATC gave me quarters in a little shack so close to the runway that the C-54's had to detour to keep from creasing my pillow. I'd wake up every morning about 4 A.M., which was when the C-54's started leaving for Guadalcanal and Honolulu. They'd taxi down the runway, turn, test each of the four motors and then give them the gun, and the way they'd come zooming at my little house, with those four engines chewing the air, made my hair stand up like Southern Democrats voting against the poll tax. Those big planes used to swoop by so close that if the guy at the controls swerved just a little, I'd go with him. Naturally, that worried me because I wasn't packed.

We did two shows on Canton. One for the Army and one for the Navy. But it was at the Army show that Frances was singing "I'm in the Mood for Love" and a kid in the back row hollered, "Sister, you came to the right spot!"

I'd twisted my wrist in that ball game on Christmas, so I had my wrist strapped. And after the poker game, with some Seabees, that I got into on Canton, I was completely strapped.

But you don't mind posing in that South Pacific climate. It's so warm, who needs pants!

And having asked the question, "Who needs pants?" I'll answer it . . . about five million exservicemen.

Eye doctors reported an epidemic of people complaining of spots before their eyes. And after looking into the cause, they decided that the only way to end the epidemic was to forbid veterans to wear their jungle clothes on the streets.

South Sea Island Makeshift

Some of the men shopping for clothes in Hollywood had a little trouble. They were so used to getting their stuff from a supply sergeant that the clerks had to throw the suits on the floor before they could get the guys to try them on. One of them climbed into the first civilian suit he'd worn in four years and the padding in the coat almost drove him crazy. He kept twisting and ducking all over the store, trying to shake the MP's hand off his shoulder.

Little habits like that are hard to abandon. A Marine who'd spent three and a half years fighting Japs in the jungle must have been slightly touched by his experiences, because, when the clerk handed him a tweed coat to try on, he spent three quarters of an hour searching through the fuzz for snipers.

There really was a terrible shortage. Conditions actually got so bad that things like this happened. A Navy flier was trying on a brown suit. Hardly any alteration was needed on the coat and the ensign seemed thoroughly satisfied with the way the pants fit. But the clerk said, "Don't you think the trousers are a little large around the seat?" And the tail gunner stuck his head out and said, "Mind your own business. *I* need room, too."

Actually, civilian clothes had a lot to do with re-enlistment. I did a show for a bunch of men who were just about to be released, so I started out by saying, "Look, fellas, here's the kind of clothes you'll be wearing when you get out." And fifty men immediately re-enlisted. Some sailors said they'd re-enlist if the uniform was changed. They wanted a patch in the hatch. Other guys figured it was easier to stay in the Navy than to try to get out of those pants.

Maybe it was the discomfort of those tight pants that made all Navy personnel so interested in getting every last little

So This Is Peace

bit of comfort possible under battle conditions. I know that one of the most sympathetic hunks of brass I ever met was a Navy man, Admiral Jones. I never met anyone more considerate of entertainers. If there's ever a "next time," I'd like to have Admiral Jones handle all the details.

After we did our first show on Tarawa, the Admiral invited us to see the official moving pictures of the Battle of Tarawa. It

South Sea Island Makeshift

was back area by that time. But it was sensational to sit on that beach which men had fought over and watch the pictures of their bloody struggle as the big planes took off for the new forward area . . . Saipan. The noise they made going out and the news they brought coming in just added to the big, big bang it gave us to realize that we were actually able to watch victory being won.

Then they showed us some of the things that made the going tough there on Tarawa, strong points that were actually pillboxes inside of pillboxes. In these the Jap used British weapons he had captured at Singapore. Those weapons must be all over the United States by now. Every soldier had one. What souvenir scroungers! One of the pillboxes had a Diesel engine in it. And when the Seabees wanted to put the engine back in commission, they had to forage all over the island to beg back parts from the soldiers.

During the last show we did on Tarawa, a little mouse ran along a wire that stretched over the heads of the men, from the projection booth to the stage. The biggest laugh in the show was when I tried to get the mouse away so it wouldn't frighten the girls and a Seabee hollered, "Ah, leave the mouse alone. He's looking for a hunk o' cheese and thinks you're Bing."

It was right after we left Tarawa that I bombed the Japs. Instead of an Oak Leaf Cluster, I was awarded a poison-ivy branch.

We were heading for Kwajalein and passed over an island called Millie which was still being held by the Nips. Our forces had by-passed it on our leap-frog route to Tokyo. Naturally, those Japs on their isolated little hunk of Hirohito's hoked-up empire were really on forced Diet A. So just to help their food situation, we dropped down to 10,000 feet, opened the bomb-bay doors, and dropped some milk bottles . . . empty ones, of course.

Falling at high speed, those bottles made the same siren-pitched sound characteristic of a high-explosive shell. I personally didn't feel too happy about this milk-bottle bombardment because those monkeys still had "ack-ack" and they might've wanted to start playing "Keep Those Bottles Quiet." But nothing happened, so I guess they didn't have enough ammo to waste on actors.

We met quite a lot of fancy brass on Kwajalein. General Hale, head of the Seventh Air Force, gave us each a medallion of Saint Joseph, Patron Saint of Fliers. Captain Gillespie of the Navy gave us his house. And General Landon gave us that feeling you get when you're near someone who has touched destiny. General Landon was the man who was bringing those B-17's into Pearl on December 7. There was cellophane still covering his guns and they had to fly around waiting for the Japs to stop strafing the runway before they could land. Nice sensation. But that Saint Joseph's medal was one of those little gifts you feel good about. Specially when you're flying around in soup so thick it's got clams in it.

One of the first spots they took us to after our first show on Kwaj. was the landing barge on the beach that a Navy surgeon had turned over and used as a dressing station while the first assault waves were still coming ashore. There were so many guys in such bad shape he just couldn't handle any of them on the beach without the protection of that barge. Many a guy got fixed up under that landing barge and went right back into the war. And if a guy didn't go back it wasn't because those doctors didn't do all they could.

The turned-over boat reminded me of a story both officers and men were telling all over the Pacific—behind their hands. According to the yarn, Nimitz and MacArthur were coming ashore in a Navy launch when it capsized. After the two five-star finals were fished out, Nimitz said to MacArthur, "I hope you won't let my men hear that I can't swim." MacArthur said, "Trust me as long as you don't let my men hear that I can't walk on the water."

While on Kwaj. we had a little laundry done by the men, who'd rigged up washing machines. They were sort of Rube Goldberg inventions, featuring a barrel with an arrangement of paddles in it driven by a windmill. The soldiers just turned these toward the nearest Marine barracks, which kept the windmills spinning, and got their laundry done without scrubbing.

Also, while we were on Kwajalein, the Armed Forces Radio setup, Colonel Tom Lewis' outfit, had us do a trailer for the men on Saipan telling them we were coming. Naturally, after this we expected to find the island deserted when we arrived. But it wasn't. That Army discipline really works.

So This Is Peace

And so did Tom's AFRS. Every place we went in the Pacific we heard Armed Forces Radio Service shows bringing a little bit of home to the men. Anything a guy wanted to hear, they'd give him on "Command Performance." And some of the guys wanted to hear some sensational things. There was a request to hear the sizzling of a steak broiled by Lana Turner. So they actually recorded the sound of a steak being broiled by Lana Turner. I was on that show, too. I happened to be standing between the steak and Lana. So I got broiled on both sides.

All over the Pacific islands we kept running into people we knew. On Eniwetok we did two shows and after one of them a guy passed me in the dark and hollered, "Hi, Bob!"

I said, "Hya, kid." Next morning I found out it was Henry Fonda, a lieutenant on Admiral Hoover's staff.

As we were coming into Eniwee, some B-24's were returning from a raid on Truk. We were ordered to fly around and let them land first. Some had injured aboard. But none of them seriously, we learned later. Just some guys knocked out by the concussion from near misses at 20,000 feet over Truk. That's all!

Of course all those "ack-ack" shots fired at our planes over Truk were not near misses. There were plenty of planes shot down. And while many a man didn't come back, the Navy actually snatched survivors right out of Truk while it was still the Japs' greatest naval base.

A PBY Catalina patrol bomber picked up two fliers who'd been floating around among the Jap ships in Truk roadstead for days. At night they could lie on their rubber raft and just be quiet and pray. But during the day they had to turn the raft upside down, with the blue side up, so the yellow side wouldn't be so conspicuous. Snatching these guys out of that

South Sea Island Makeshift

trap was a wonderful job of air-sea rescue work. And one of the kids saved later said, "I'd like to meet the guy who gave me that first cup of hot coffee. I'd marry him."

Other Hollywood fighters on Eniwetok were Hal Cantor, then writing for Armed Forces Radio, now writing for Don Ameche; and Bob Kepka, who used to be with Paramount and was a photographer for the Seabees. We did a show for a lot of those Seabees, and one of them hollered, "Hey, Bob, I read in your book, *I Never Left Home*,* that the Seabees are the boys who build what the Marines land on."

"You're not kicking at that kind of billing, are you?" I asked.

"No," the guy said, "but now we have more important work out here! Now we're building the roads the Japs retreat over." It's almost the truth!

They gave us a fighter escort of Corsairs from Eniwee to Engebi, where we did a show and then ducked down to Majuro, where they had signs up all over, "Welcome, Jack Benny." "Welcome, Fibber McGee." "Welcome, Fred Allen." But we didn't care. Because Captain Bob Grant of the Navy welcomed us with food. That man likes nice victuals and gave us such a dinner of green turtle soup in sherry, filet mignon, salad, green peas, and ice cream that we thought we had a direct wire to Chasen's and Romanoff's.

On Majuro I got my first Pacific haircut at Mike's Barber Shop—"New York Style Haircuts." I think he cut it a little close around the East Bronx. What a clipping I got! I've had my ears set out before. But that was the first time I took them home in a sack. Mike dropped a high bowl on my low forehead and let himself go. And when he took off the bowl, my head looked as if he'd left some shredded wheat in it.

---

* PUBLISHER'S NOTE: It's not too late. Still 75,000 copies left.

I also had a little work done on the other end. I mean I went to the hospital to have my fungus treated. As Bert Lahr would say, "Some fungus, eh, kid?" One morning I looked down and found a little jungle growing under my feet. When I tried to step out of it, I saw it was growing *out* of my feet. It was a very common sort of thing in that area, so I had it. I didn't want to miss anything. And I didn't. The nurses at the hospital were all very pretty. I wanted to stay on Majuro a little longer, but the nurses were all RN's . . rather not.

So the next morning we walked over the ground of Makin Island, sacred to the memory of Carlson's raiders. And we went right to work doing a show in a coconut grove, but we couldn't find Freddy Martin.

As we wandered around, we were warned not to laugh at any of the women. The guys said the native chief didn't mind if you took pictures of the gals bathing in the nude, but he objected if you laughed at them. And most of those chicks were good for a laugh. While we were there, one soldier wanted to take a few quick ones of a native beauty wearing even less than the travel posters promise. She objected strenuously and asked the guy please to wait until she put on something. He was disappointed, but he waited while she ran into her shack and a moment later came back wearing a red band tied around her head. That red band looked very formal. Most of the girls just wore towels around their heads. Most of the towels said "Hamilton Field."

And Hamilton Field was where I wished I'd stayed when we arrived on Bougainville in the middle of an artillery duel. There was a lot of that tossing of HE shells back and forth. And there was a story going around the island about a guy who always used to start praying when the shells began to fall. He'd go right down on his knees and say, "God save me! God save me!"

Finally his sergeant couldn't stand it any longer and hollered, "Don't be so doggoned selfish. Pray for all of us."

Naturally, we spent a very happy, restful night on Bougainville, listening to our artillery lob shells into Jap positions beyond the perimeter, which happened to be about 10,000 yards from our tent. The idea was to keep Tojo's little earthworms where they belonged. If we didn't keep doing that, they'd wind up in our chow lines. You never knew where they might be. One night on Bougainville I had to leave my tent after dark. And before I got where I was going, a vine hit me in the neck and scared me so I didn't finish the trip. I thought one of the little Sons of Heaven had sneaked in to steal some ham.

And besides the brawling with artillery, just to keep the men from getting too bored they had a live volcano, Mount Bagana, located right in the vicinity of our operations.

Of course on Itape we had our perimeter shrunk to seventy-five yards—and that's really shrinking—and instead of high-explosive shells to keep off the Nips, the Red Arrow Band of the 32nd Division played very loud. I preferred it on Bougainville. The music was hot but the Jap snipers were hotter.

On Bougainville we ran into a lot of old friends. An infantry division from Ohio happened to be roughing it there for a few months. And a lot of the guys knew me from Cleveland, but I managed to hush them up before they talked. But just to show how handy it is to have friends from home, Ray Tuck, of the *Cleveland Press,* saw to it that we got our laundry done. As you know, I'm an old *Press* man, too. I used to sell it.

So This Is Peace

All in all, we did nine shows on Bougainville; four of them in the rain. It rained so hard during one show I asked the guys if they wanted to call it off until later. They just yelled back in chorus, "Keep going, sissy!" Those were the days when a lot of guys didn't know how much "later" they had left.

It rained so hard, the girls had to work in their bare feet to save their shoes. But the doughfeet in the jungles really welcome the rain. It fills their barrels and they can take showers. The contraptions those guys rigged up to catch the lovely stuff from upstairs would make the average inventor green with envy. The rain made some of the men green with moss.

But I've run into some rain during peacetime, too. When we played Foreman Field, at Norfolk, Va., we got a little jungle rain. Foreman Field is the football stadium of William and Mary College. And we had the place jammed. There was a lot of Navy brass from the Naval Station at Norfolk, the Governor was there, and everything would have been great but just after we started the show those great big king-size drops began to fall.

It was kind of funny to see the Governor using an officer's chair for an umbrella and two admirals and a captain holding a bench over their heads to keep the rain from melting the scrambled eggs on their caps. The rest of the audience ducked under the stadium, to wait for the rain to stop. But pretty soon it was clear that it wasn't going to clear.

It began to look as if we'd have to give back a lot of dough to the paying customers when someone told me about a field house connected with the stadium, and when I ducked over there to see how many people it would hold I found a couple of hundred kids taking an exam. They were sitting in these

South Sea Island Makeshift

one-armed lunchroom chairs. And there was a teacher at a desk, watching them.

She held her finger to her lips for silence, so I started to whisper. But one of the kids got a gander at my prow and before long we'd talked teacher into taking an hour-and-a-half recess and letting the kids see a free show.

So everybody from under the stadium piled into the field house, plus a lot of little kids who sneaked in. The joint was really jammed, with the Governor and the Navy brass well back in the balcony.

I told them how the soldiers on Bougainville hadn't minded a little rain. And after the show one of the guys who was taking the exam told me he'd been on Bougie when we were there and was now finishing his schooling under the GI Bill of Rights.

We ran into one of my favorite Brown Derby waiters, Al Sanchez, on Bougainville. I said, "How's it going, Al?"

"Tips are falling off," he said.

But a guy in his outfit told me about being up front with Al during some machine-gun activity. His captain called Al and ordered: "Run back and bring some 20-mm. shells."

Al ran back and returned with 16-mm.'s.

The captain looked at them and said, "I thought I told you to get 20's."

The ex-Brown Derby waiter knew the answer to that. "Listen, Captain," he said, "don't you know there's a war going on?"

All right, so it isn't true, but it's typical. I think I missed my big chance to get ahead on Bougainville. After we left, someone told me there were head-hunters on the island. I might have been able to make a trade.

Besides newspapermen, actors, and waiters, I ran into Bob

So This Is Peace

Garred, CBS announcer, Rev. Father Duffy of Chicago, and Major Joe Foss, the modest man with the Congressional Medal, on a little island that must remain nameless because I've forgotten the name of it.

And on Treasury Island I ran into Light Horse Harry Wilson, who used to pack plenty of pigskin for the Point. Those fliers in Harry Wilson's group really looked up to me. They spent all afternoon looking up to me. I'd like to catch the wise guy who fastened my suspenders to the tail of a P-61.

Harry also took me for a ride in a South Pacific Canoe... Air Corps Style. That's two P-38 belly tanks lashed together. We had a lovely swim. It would have been even more fun if I'd known how to swim. But we did three shows on Treasury with a lot of help from a wonderful Negro band. It was nice working on Treasury, the Treasury's been working on me for so long.

On Espiritu Santos, we were going through the wards after a show and came across a kid getting a transfusion. "Are they giving you the raspberry?" I said. He smiled and answered, "Yeah, and it feels good, too." A couple of hours later his CO said, "You know that boy you saw getting a transfusion? He died." The memory of that kid's face and his courage and the many similar memories are enough reasons for feeling there must never be another war.

I began to get a little worried that the USO didn't like our act when suddenly people began telling me that Jack Benny was also traveling in the same area. He's such a go-getter. No distance was too far for him to go to sell a few cigarettes. Actually, I think he was selling Grape Nuts at the time. Maybe he didn't make his quota in the Pacific, so General Foods let him go. But Jack had a fine unit, I hate myself for writing.

How could he miss with Larry Adler, Martha Tilton, June Bruner, and Carole Landis, the girl who really brings it with her? June Bruner was so good I took her away from the sordid atmosphere of a Jack Benny troupe the following year, to make the trip to Germany with me... as you'd know if you'd been reading carefully up to here.

Judith Anderson was also playing the area at the same time we were. We followed her into a lot of spots. It was sort of from *Hamlet* to Ham. Only an artist like Anderson could have made those GI's like *Macbeth* in the jungle.

In the New Guinea area at Hollandia, which could have been called Bulldozer Junction, we got a load of how those mechanical Martha Rayes renovated the town. They were run by the Seabees, who did a terrific job of clearing the way for those essential supplies that *had* to keep moving toward the front. When we played the hospital, we met Lew Ayres as well as Bud Ward, the national amateur golf champion, who was then in the Air Force. Lew wouldn't come up on the stage and take a bow even when his own gang gave him a terrific ovation. Dr. Kildare in khaki was strictly a soldier. And a good one.

On Munda we did some shows with the help of Clark Dennis, who used to tenor for Paul Whiteman, and Billy Sherman, of Cleveland, who warbled for Abe Lyman.

And we did one show in that area that wasn't scheduled. Our little band of gypsies flew over to the island of Pavuvu, in Piper Cubs, to do a show for the men of the 1st Marine Division then training for the invasion of Palau.

They had to take us in Pipers because the island had no regular air strip. We had to land on the road. And as we buzzed the baseball field it was the most exciting thing that happened on the trip to see those 15,000 guys all looking up and cheering each little plane as she came in. Forty per cent of those Marines were never seen again. And I ran into a bunch of the "lucky" sixty per cent in a hospital in Oakland. I happened to be going through a ward when a guy suddenly hollered, "Pavuvu!"

I tingle all over just thinking about it as I write. All the men in that ward were from the 1st Marine Division. And remeeting them was just as exciting as doing the show for them that day on Pavuvu. Because that was the day those

South Sea Island Makeshift

Marines were celebrating the second anniversary of their landing on Guadalcanal.

And they set up plenty of clatter when they caught sight of Patty T. and Frances L. Arnold Johnson, a 1st Mariner, once an NBC photographer, got it all.

Those men had been isolated on that island for nearly six months. Their walls were so covered with pinups, the termites were drooling. One guy had a picture of Betty Grable on the wall. I said, "Don't you know Grable's married to Harry James?"

The guy answered, "Who cares! After the war, we're going to kill all the buglers."

CHAPTER 8

From Bad to Würst

OF COURSE as soon as the war was over, they started closing the camps. I volunteered to help, but they didn't think I had the experience. They were mistaken. I've closed many a place.

As little as two weeks after V-J Day, I went to a camp and found it closed. I never found out how they knew I was coming. It was really an eerie sight. Like one of those Western ghost towns. There was nothing at all left of the camp but a skeleton lying in the street. It must have been a sergeant. His mouth was still open. Finally I found a civilian watchman, huddled by a stove. I said to him, "When they close these camps, does everybody get shipped out?"

He said, "Everybody but the bugler. And they'd ship him out, too, if they could get anybody to dig him up."

This checks with what the guy told me on that island in the Pacific.

I happened to be in Germany on V-J Day and naturally there was a lot of excitement there. So I could hardly wait to get home and see how things had changed in the States. The very moment I walked into the house I could tell the war was over. There was Grandpa sitting in his old place by the radiator, reading his release from the Dodgers.

Naturally, we went right to work playing Separation Centers. Separation Center, that's an Army term meaning, "Let's push them around just once more before we let them go home." And just to get an idea what the men did and talked about on their way to one of those centers, I accompanied a bunch of them home on a troop train. Troop train, that's another Army term meaning "basic training on wheels."

But it really was an unusual train. You've heard of the Twentieth Century Limited? Well, a troop train is the Spike Jones arrangement of it. I had a seat with a guy who had several big bumps on his head.

I said, "Did you have an accident?"

He said, "No. I slept on top of the pile and during the night the guy on the bottom got the hiccups."

I said I sat next to this guy. That's not quite right. They have a different kind of seating arrangement on troop trains. For instance, if you want to play cards, the guy who has the seat deals, the fellow on his lap picks up the cards, and the guy on top plays them.

Of course, troop trains also have a different kind of air conditioning. You open the windows. And that way a man can really pick up plenty of bituminous. One sergeant got so much coal dust in his ears he had to sign a contract with John L. Lewis before he could clean them out.

There was one WAC on the train and shortly after it went through a tunnel she was wearing a charm bracelet featuring six battle stars, four Distinguished Service Crosses, eight silver bars, and a private's ear.

Every time the train butcher passed through the cars, those GI's, who'd really learned how to swap things while in the

Army, went to work on him. In five hundred miles they traded him out of his suit, sold him eight dollars' worth of French postcards, and a low-point man adopted four of his kids. But the low-point men after V-J Day had relatively little to worry about. They knew they'd be getting out alive.

I saw some of the outfits coming home to the States, headed for redistribution centers, while the war was still on. Redistribution Center, that's still another Army term meaning "caught with your points down." Then was the time low-point men were really worried. But high or low . . . when they came off the boat . . . well, the bunch I saw getting off the boat hardly seemed to touch their feet to the gangplank. Come to think of it, there wasn't any gangplank. They just laid down a top sergeant and walked over him. But what different attitudes the guys in those redistribution centers had! The ones coming in sometimes kissed the dirt. And the ones shipping out kicked it in their faces.

Of course, the guys brought back a lot of things from overseas. One GI even tried to smuggle his wife from Australia. He would have made it, too. But one night the MP's caught him kissing his barracks bag good night.

As I was saying, the moment I got home after V-J Day, I could tell the war was over. My brother was discharged from the Army.

Naturally, being my brother got him a lot of breaks in the Army. But they all healed nicely. He was in the artillery in charge of one of the big guns. Well, he wasn't exactly in charge of a big gun. Every morning he sprayed the gardenia on his second lieutenant's lapel with a water pistol. He was discharged as a PNC. That's a Psycho Neurotic Chowhound. But don't think he didn't do a great job in the war. He was in the Air Force and brought down five planes . . . all his own. But he was in there fighting every minute.

From Bad to Würst

He didn't get out quite as quickly as we expected he would. It turned out that he'd forged so many three-day passes he'd forgotten his real name. But he was in four years, which is a long time for a Republican.

The very first thing he did when he got out was to mail the MP's a phonograph record telling them exactly what he thought of them. But I heard that when they tried to play it, the needle melted. There was one little unhappy incident connected with my brother's return from the Army. He broke the cook's heart the first night he was home for dinner. When she opened the dining-room door, he rushed in so fast he knocked her over, sat down, ate everything in sight, scraped his plate off on the floor, and then walked into the kitchen and sneered, "Officers getting all the good food, I suppose!"

But he soon got back to normal, eight bottles of beer a day. He was hit pretty bad when they had to restrict the amount of grain the brewers could use. It wasn't that he needed the beer so much. But collecting and taking back those big bottles was his main source of income. Of course he wasn't really allergic to the beer, either. I guess he'd have liked it in Bremen, where they gave away eight per cent beer free to American servicemen. I really didn't think it compared with American beer, but Colonna strained plenty of it through his hedge.

He guzzled so much beer he finally came over to me and said, "Drop everything, Hope!"

"Why, Colonna?"

"Take my hat off!"

"Why, Colonna?"

"Don't stand there asking questions! Blow the foam off my head!"

While we were in town, the Burgomaster issued a radio statement to the people of the city. He said, and I quote, "Ve must all ged togedder and luff our goot friens, der American schvine!" Unquote. So we had a guard.

He was Private Shig Morishige, who was wounded three times while fighting with the tough Japanese-American 442d Regiment in Italy. All he talked about was going home to Denver. One morning we heard a machine gun firing outside and rushed downstairs.

Shig was standing with a BAR in his hand. And there was a Nazi battle flag at his feet.

"What's the matter?" I shouted.

"Nothing," said Shig.

"Why the shooting?"

"I just liberated this Nazi battle flag and I wanted to make it look a little more battle-worn," he explained.

We heard a lot of talk about how bad Russian looting was.

From Bad to Würst

But our boys liberated plenty of merchandise, too: binoculars, cameras, and small arms of all kinds. One guy even tried to get away with a Tiger Tank. But the MP's made me put it back.

So This Is Peace

**Using Bremen as headquarters, we fanned out over plenty of Reich, playing to guys in bandstands, beer gardens, and cow pastures. I say cow pastures because most of the time, traveling by jeep, we seemed to be riding across them. Once they rushed us from Vegesack to Nordenham by extra-fast jeep. Fast jeep ... that's Betty Hutton with four-wheel transmission. What a ride! I'd heard about the famous German *Autobahn*. But the only roads we hit were eight feet wide and made out of lumpy bricks. I considered giving up jeep riding. After the first mile over those German roads, I felt paralyzed from the hips down. After the second mile, the jeep started complaining.

About twenty-three shell holes north of Bremen is the Bremerhaven Naval Compound, and it's a spot they really compounded. It took one big going over. The RAF went over it just once, but with one thousand planes. They arrived and left Bremerhaven in twenty-seven minutes ... flat!

Most of our audiences in Bremerhaven were sailors. Those are guys who have claustrophobia from the waist down. And in Bremerhaven, as in the U. S. A., the Navy was devoted to life, happiness, and the pursuit of liberty. But we always find it quite different working before the Navy. When the girls come on the stage, a soldier puts his fingers in his mouth and whistles through his teeth. A sailor puts his whole hand in his mouth and whistles through his ears.

After the show they drove us around a little. We saw the old German luxury liner, *Europa,* with an American prize crew aboard. And then they took us out to the local country club. The Krauts had a nine-hole golf course, but none of the Nazis were ever very good golf players. It's too tough to drive a ball with one hand stuck up in the air.

The club was under the management of Uncle Sam, with**

From Bad to Würst

PFC Hermann Kramm of Pittsburgh's Slippery Rock Country Club as the pro. Any GI who wanted to knock off a couple of rounds could get clubs, balls, and a few lessons from Kramm, all for nothing. He corrected one of my mistakes. The mistake was the idea that I, too, could get some free lessons.

One thing that killed the girls while driving around Bremen and Bremerhaven was the fancy uniforms worn by the German traffic cops. The Krauts have always gone for gold braid, but those *gnädige* gendarmes looked like the whole wardrobe from a Shubert musical, with legs. Every policeman was the Chocolate Soldier, but with almonds. They were the only people I ever saw who looked as if they outranked a Park Avenue doorman.

On our last day in Bremen, we had breakfast in the Bremen Rathskeller, which had become the BPC Mess. The Rathskeller is over four hundred years old, sort of an underground Brown Derby with cobwebs instead of Bob Cobb. The walls are all decorated with murals of fat characters chasing even fatter blondes. And all of them seemed to have mislaid their clothing ration books.

They also took us into subbasements where there were great big carved wine casks that were so old they had to keep them full all the time or they'd collapse. I could say we have the identical thing in Hollywood, but it wouldn't be a nice remark to make about W. C. Fields.

But this ancient spot was strictly GI and run by Pvt. Bert Parish, the chowhounds' delight. Before the war he was half owner of New York's Hickory House restaurant and turned out such food in that German basement that the termites were coming out of the walls and making table reservations.

After breakfast they took us to Bad Kissingen. That's the

name of a place, not the description of a girl with a weak pucker. I tried that joke out on our pilot, Lt. George McKellar, and he didn't think it was funny, either.

We were a little late in leaving Bremen because we had to go back three times to get some of the equipment we'd forgotten. We all had to carry our own toilet stuff, my creams and lotions, and it's really very funny to check out of a hotel and steal your own towels and soap.

The ship that took us away from Bremen was called *Halfpint Nan*. I never knew why. But after a couple of years away from home, a silly name, and the sentimental memory of a woman that goes with it, become awfully important.

At Bad Kissingen we stayed at the press camp, which had formerly been a sanatorium. The bellboys all wore white coats and kept looking at me and murmuring, "Ah, reconversion has set in."

Bad, of course, means bath, and Bad Kissingen is sort of a Bavarian Saratoga Springs where the Krauts used to flock to soak in the mineral water. I tested some of it, and, believe me, it will never replace the old-fashioned mickey. I hadn't smelled anything like it before. But when I started playing colleges, I ran into that Bad Kissingen water smell in all the better chemistry labs. I always spent a few hours in a chemistry lab, making a little gin and things.

There were a lot of other mineral springs around Bad Kissingen, so we went from bad to bad. At Bad Neustadt we poked a little fun at a bunch of the guys in the 9th Air Force There were a lot of displaced persons around, listening to the show. Poles, Slavs, Russians, Greeks, and Belgians. They didn't understand much of what was said, but when anyone else laughed, they laughed. So I signed a bunch of them to thirteen-week contracts for my postwar broadcast audience.

From Bad to Würst

It turned out that the military governor of Bad Kissingen was an old friend of mine, Capt. Merle Potter, who was dramatic critic on the Minneapolis *Journal* when I was murdering vaudeville and vice versa.

At Merle's office I met the ex-Kaiser's grandson, Prince Louis Ferdinand, and his wife, Princess Kyra. Louis had been to Hollywood long enough to imitate Von Stroheim. He spoke English well enough and had become quite an eager beaver about being friends with our side. He kept himself busy arranging boar hunts and band concerts for "the brave Americans." He didn't fool anybody.

Colonna and I sat with Capt. Potter while he held court. They were kind of short on members of the Bar Association, so Merle was not only judge but jury, and both attorneys. He'd say to the defendant, "I ought to make you sit through Bob Hope's show." It's remarkable what a lot of justice a good man can deal out.

I don't know what I could have done to make Merle dislike me, but Major Johnny Hatch of Decatur, Georgia, the CO of the 428th Fighter Squadron, phoned me and said,

"Capt. Potter though you might like a ride in a Droop-Snoot. Do you want to go?"

I said, "Sure." Next day I had my head examined. A Droop-Snoot is the Jimmy Durante of P-38's, a fighter with the armament removed and a glass-enclosed seat stuck right in the nose. Sitting in that greenhouse makes riding on the cowcatcher of a roller coaster seem like a siesta. It's riding on the handle bars of a bicycle being pedaled by Superman. We really traveled unbelievably fast. I know because I opened my eyes once to look.

I'd met Johnny Hatch's father in the South Pacific, and every time Johnny took me into one of those vertical dives, I'd start wishing his old man had remained a bachelor. It was the first time I'd ever been in a vertical dive, although I'd come out of several dives horizontal.

We were scheduled to do a show in Schweinfurt, so Johnny landed me there. I just had time to sort my blood back into the right veins before the rest of the troop arrived in a C-47.

After the show we had lunch at the EM Mess and I bumped into another guy from Hollywood, Sergeant Bill Clelland.

From Bad to Würst

Bill was pretty discouraged. He was the weatherman at the Schweinfurt air strip but he wasn't doing his job right and he knew it.

"Honest, Bob," he told me, "no matter what the instruments say, it's tough for a guy from Hollywood to predict rain."

A cute little Russian DP who worked in the sanatorium did our laundry for us and I spent fifteen minutes trying to convince her that she ought to take some money for the work.

But all Olga would do was shake her head and say, "No. No. I do it gladly as a favor for the fine artist."

And Colonna thought I was crazy when I told her our unit was the Don Cossacks. Imagine what the Cossacks would have thought if they'd heard Colonna. Olga did a swell job of washing and ironing. But I still can't figure out how she got the iron to scorch a picture of Stalin in all my shirts.

At Erlangen we put up in a broken-down little hotel that reminded me of my vaudeville days. There was only one bath in the place and that was always taken. It was the kind of hotel in which some forgotten comic of the six-a-day invented the joke, "Have you taken a bath today?" Answer: "Why, is there one missing?"

But we were truly grateful for the hot water, and Colonna, Pepper, Price, Mike Cullen, and a couple of characters who just wandered in off the street were all trying to get into the tub at once. . . . After we got cleaned up, they flew us to Darmstadt, to do a show for the 415th, P-61 night fighter, Squadron.

Between the acts, I got to talking with Capt. Max Gilstrap and Lt. Hank Long, advisory editors of the German edition of *Stars and Stripes*.

So This Is Peace

Everywhere we went in the ETO we found the guys reading one of the five editions of *S & S* (that's *not* Simon and Schuster) and everywhere they had a lot of respect for it.

The German edition ran to about 200,000 copies, printed on the presses of the once famous *Frankfurter Zeitung*. And the editorial offices were over a big brewery. It got so they had to have a man standing by every morning to blow the suds off the first 300 copies. Capt. Gilstrap told me that they operated in that brewery in Frankfurt for over three months before someone pulled up a trap door and discovered the whole business was located over a huge, underground plant that had been turning out Opal engines.

From Darmstadt we went to Fürth, and did an hour or so of stuff for the HQ men of the 10th Tactical Reconnaissance Group, a P-51 Mustang fighter squadron. The first thing I saw when I landed was a Mustang with a picture of me and *Shovelsnoot* painted across the nose.

My attorneys are still trying to contact the pilot, Lt. E. L. Kenny. I'd have dealt with him myself, but he was a pretty big guy, and I wanted to see Berlin with *both* eyes.

Coming into Berlin, we landed at Tempelhof Airfield, were rushed off the plane, and were on a stage playing before the 301st Troop Carrier Squadron before our ears stopped popping.

As soon as the show was over and the soldiers moved out, the whole area began to swarm with German civilians scrambling around the grass for cigarette butts. It made me kind of sore. My USO contract said I was to have that concession.

For our second show in Berlin, we played for the men of the First and Eighty-second Airborne Armies at the Berlin Telefunken Building, after which they gave us a fine lunch. It was such a great spread that after it was over we went back into the kitchen to shake hands with the cooks and do a few jokes for the men who'd been too busy preparing our food to see our show. Maybe it was best we didn't play for them till after the lunch. The food was delicious.

Our third show on the first day in Berlin was in a real theater that had somehow survived our air forces. It was Berlin's famous old Titiania Palast. I hadn't seen a curtain in so long that when I went on stage I thought it was a shower bath and started looking for the faucets.

While driving between shows we got a gander at Berlin. A lot of the architecture was modern. A lot was missing. When they rebuild the city it'll be even more modern. To lovers of traditional architecture that may be the most horrible result of the war the Germans have to face. Who can tell what German architects may come up with in the way of modern design? Let's hope they get a better architect than Hitler.

We'd thought Bremen was kaput. Bremen turned out to be just a sort of Berlin (JG). Almost every house in Berlin had at least a few holes in the roof from falling flak. The town was completely beat, and the people, too, looked thoroughly beaten; much more so than any of the other Germans we'd seen.

It wasn't hard to understand why, either. Our fliers had made Berlin into a rock pile, a sort of down payment on what we hoped would be the security of London, New York, Chicago, and Moscow. It was a down payment, all right. Really down!

Moving around Berlin, as in Bremen, I found it strange that I got such an emotional smash out of utter destruction. But I guess I was thinking of the guys who'd gone, the men who went to help do the job. And I couldn't help feeling proud of men who'd given so much to throw their answer at bigotry, hatred, greed, and intolerance.

Generally, happiness goes with pride. But the proudness I felt gazing at broken Berlin was different. I couldn't be glad. And yet I couldn't be sorry. I wanted to be human, to forgive and forget. And yet in my heart I found it hard even to think of forgiving them for the men I couldn't forget.

While touring Berlin we frequently drove over peculiar-looking cases embedded in the streets. I turned to PFC Mario Romano, of Chicago, our driver, and asked, "What are those?"

"Duds," he said casually.

"You mean those shells are live?" I asked.

"Who knows?" he said, as we drove over another. "They haven't had time to remove them yet."

"Then they might explode," I shrieked.

"Any minute," he answered.

I'll bet the reason they hadn't been removed was because the guy who had to do the work was looking around for a rubber shovel.

I got up early the morning of our second day in Berlin

and went out to the big park north of the Brandenburg Gate, near the junction of the British, Russian, and American sectors. The huge evergreen trees were all chopped off and stripped by bombs and artillery fire. And I understand they were sawed up for firewood to keep freezing Berlin warm in the winter of 1945–1946. Here thousands of people formed a surging mass that crossed the walkways and boiled around the bomb craters. It was Berlin's Black Market.

The people were mostly German civilians with a few Russian and British soldiers and GI's. Everyone had something to sell. Women featured clocks, linen, and jewelry. Men had knapsacks filled with cameras, film, postcards, and anything they thought anyone might buy.

There was a local joke that if you wanted to know what time it was you had to ask a Russian. Because the Russians bought a lot of wrist watches from our guys at prices ranging from $300 to $1000.

I tried but I couldn't get a wire through to the Elgin people.

The whole combination of the broken trees, the broken buildings in the background, and the broken people milling around, trying to sell what was left of their broken lives to their conquerors, should have been photographed and shown to the German people every few weeks. It might have helped.

Of course I ran down to Potsdam for the Big Three conference. I ran down because I couldn't get any transportation. I sent in my name and they sent out the MP's. That conference was so private even the sentries had sentries. So we put on a show in the Hollywood of Germany, a place near Potsdam called Babelsberg. We did the show on a big sound stage filled with men from the First and Eighty-second Airborne Armies and the 713th MP Battalion, which was doing police work around Potsdam and Berlin. There was so much brass around that every street corner looked like the back row in Harry James' band. Backstage at the Titiania Palast, during our second show, Joseph E. Davies, Frank Murphy, and Major General Parks were only three of the men I ran into. They all stepped aside.

Of course our troupe had dinner at the VIP Mess. VIP ... that's Army talk for Very Important Persons. But they make exceptions. I was told that, considering my inexperience, I served very nicely. It was Patty Thomas' birthday. So they had a big cake, which she hacked up with a gold-plated Nazi sword.

Sitting at the next table to us were W. Averell Harriman, General Hall, General Estabrook, and Admiral Cook. We had quite a talk. I said, "Hello."

They turned to each other and said, "Who's he?"

The most pleasant surprise of the evening was running into Pvt. Frank Risotto, the ETO Sinatra. He may even become the ETO Crosby if he can manage to make the age. Last time I'd seen Frank was when his band played for our show at the Odeon Theater in London in 1943. The band and Frank's tonsils were still very solid.

Our last day in Berlin I had a little trouble packing. I couldn't decide which was more important to put in my suitcase: my clothes or the piece of marble from Hitler's desk, the plate from his private bomb shelter, and the stay from Eva Braun's corset. What souvenirs! Like everyone else in Berlin, I operated on a sort of lend-loot agreement.

But I've since found out that civilians and enlisted men may make like an occasional Leica, but they can't compete with a colonel and a WAC captain. That's an unbeatable combination, unless you are Tiffany's. On June 11 and 12,

From Bad to Würst

when our little Airborne Vaudeville Troupe tapped the tills in Oakland and San Francisco, I spent the night at the Palace. That was the first time I couldn't sleep in the Palace. A colonel kept prowling through my room, looking for jewels.

I got the Hitler stuff on a last-minute, quick tour of inspection. We saw what was left of the Hotel Adlon and the Reichstag and ended up at the Reichskanzlei, Hitler's business office, which was the scene of a very bitter last-ditch battle between the SS men and the Russians.

So This Is Peace

Although it looked more or less intact, that joint was really messed up. Artillery and small-arms fire had knocked holes in nearly all the walls, and the rooms had been cleared of everything portable by souvenir-hunting British, Russian, and American soldiers who came through the place daily on sight-seeing tours just like the one we were on. In Germany, sight-seeing was a word meaning pick up anything you can carry.

The entire Chancellery was honeycombed with underground tunnels and shelters, and after getting some flashlights and climbing over broken furniture and plaster, we wound up several levels below the basement where we thought we'd found Hitler. A little Kraut was down there, with a candle as his only light, bowing and scraping and handing out Nazi insignia and mother medals. These were small bronze plaques that were given to productive *Fraus* who bore little Katzenjammers for the Reich.

On the way out of this place, we passed British Foreign Secretary Ernest Bevin and War Correspondent Louis Lochner, also doing a litle exploring. I tried to sell them the mother medal I'd bought, at a slight profit, but it was no use. Neither one of them was a mother.

When we got outside an Air Force guy who'd also been doing a little looking (Ed. note: Spell that with a *k* and not a *t*) showed us a roll of material he had under his arm and said, "I'll take this home to the States and send it to your house."

I didn't know what it was till I got home. It's one of those big Nazi swastikas you hang in front of a mass meeting. I put it up whenever my writers get together. But it's not one of those pennant flannel jobs. It's handmade tapestry with solid-

From Bad to Würst

gold fringe and would look great draped over the foot of the bed if it weren't heavier than the bed.

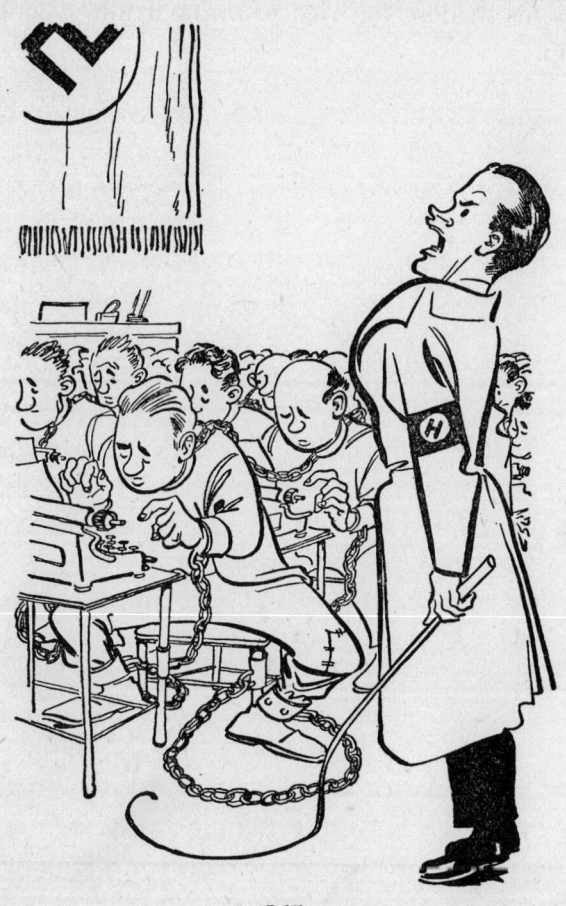

The same guy who liberated the tapestry for us got us a pass from the Russians to visit Hitler's personal air-raid shelter. It was a few hundred yards from the Chancellery, under a big garden. We went through a little door in a pillbox with walls nine feet thick and down a couple of miles of steps, and finally came out in the fanciest gopher hole I'd ever seen. It was a complete subterranean mansion with kitchens, servants' quarters, library, and a special nook for Eva . . . everything to make a paperhanger happy underground.

I'm told that after he got a look at his first B-17, Hitler spent quite a lot of time down there. In fact, the last two years of the war he only came out on Groundhog Day. And if he saw his shadow, he tried to throw it into a concentration camp.

CHAPTER 9

Deutschland unter Allies

CONCENTRATION CAMP! There are two words as frightening and terrible as those earlier two words, Spanish Inquisition.

Concentration camp! We fought to free the people slammed into those common enclosures, those corrals of human misery, for their intellectual and religious leanings. And yet, one full year after peace, those camps still exist, only their occupants are now called DP's . . . displaced persons . . . the miserable, unhappy flotsam and jetsam of war for whom there is no haven, no home, and no happiness.

In Europe, DP's are people who have been physically displaced from that part of the world in which they lived, grew up, and had their hopes. Here in the United States we have our displaced persons, too. We call them veterans.

I was shocked to learn that disabled men, totally hospitalized men, receive only twenty dollars a month from their grateful government. That sounds to me as if a soldier got a thirty-dollar cut in pay because he was careless enough to get hurt. Whatever the laws are, how can we, a rich and free people who cheered these men on to make unbelievable sacrifices, sit idly by while many of them languish in our own version—the 1946, U. S. A. version—of concentration camps, which we call hospitals, with only sixty-six cents a day to spend on necessary toilet accessories, phone calls home, smokes, sweets, reading matter, and any little presents they might want to buy, perhaps for a little son or daughter seen too seldom. They can't save much. Not at those prices. They can't even afford to join a veterans' association. There's a fight on to see that they get better. Let's hope it's won by the time this reaches you. If it's not, let's hope you'll join the fight.

And the fight's not only to see that our veterans are remembered. We have a fight to see that the war is remembered. Plenty of people are carrying on a tremendous battle to keep Americans mindful of the fact that this is the home of government "of the people, by the people, and for the people." That one race is as good as another and that any man is entitled to worship God as he sees fit.

There was a magnificent upsurge of religious feeling and understanding during the war. Men who lay in foxholes felt need for Divine understanding. People who waited at home had no outlet but to pray . . . pray for the defeat of the kind of thinking that created a world of concentration camps. I saw one of them . . . Dachau.

They told us the place had been cleaned up. But seeing the assembly-line methods that had been set up by one group of "civilized" "human beings" to slaughter another group of civilized human beings was a sickening physical shock. It was a slow type of shock that crept up on me as I went from room to room, knowing what had happened.

Deutschland unter Allies

We saw the huge room labeled "Bathroom," where the SS boys used to send the prisoners after giving them a washcloth and instructions to clean up. It had shower heads in the ceiling, but no water ever came out of them. They were dummies. The real purpose was achieved by slits in the walls through which, once the doors were bolted, poison gas was pumped.

So This Is Peace

We also saw the ovens and, standing beside them, several cans containing the ashes of American fliers who'd visited the ovens a few months before we did. There was also a sort of waiting room where living bodies were piled. The walls were bloodstained and marked in places by deep scratches made in the solid concrete by human fingernails.

This room was near the outdoor shooting gallery. Two blank walls against which thousands of prisoners of all nationalities had been machine-gunned. With typical Teutonic delicacy they allocated one wall for men, the other for women and children.

Behind these were the kennels where they kept the mad dogs that the guards turned loose among the prisoners when they wanted a few laughs. Although I saw it all with my own eyes, it was hard to believe. And I'm setting it down here because I think things like that cannot be said and resaid too many times. As soon as anyone forgets, that's how soon it can all happen again.

We were shown around Dachau by the Officer of the Day, Lt. Philip Barnes, of Chicago, and Pvt. Getzy Shiff, of Brooklyn. And we were glad to see that the stockades were already filled with SS troops guarded by men of the 45th Division who captured the camp while it was still in operation.

I talked to a lot of those 45th Division combat men and they were really rugged. Not mean. Just plain old United States Brooklyn-Chicago-Texas-Seattle tough. I was very glad to see that the SS men were in such good hands.

I was particularly pleased to see those Texans there. It wasn't hard to recognize them. You can always tell a Texan. But he'll tell you you're wrong. It must be something about the climate that makes them the way they are. The sun hangs in that Texas sky like a big fried egg, and last time I was there I asked some of the folks if it didn't bother them. "No," said one character. "It's when we start seeing bacon beside it that we begin to worry."

David Niven tells of his first experience with the fighting men of the Lone Star State. During the fighting in the Ardennes Forest his division of British and Canadian soldiers was flanked on the right by an American artillery battalion. Dave's boys had had trouble dislodging some Germans from a huge reinforced concrete pillbox and finally drove down and asked the Americans to send up some 105's to take the cement gopher hole apart. The 105's arrived in charge of a major from Texas, who quickly unlimbered his guns and started dropping the heavies on the pillbox. After a brief barrage a white flag appeared in the hands of a Prussian officer, who strode across the field, asked for the commanding officer, and faced the elongated Texan.

"Inasmuch as we are out of food," he stated through an interpreter, "my commanding officer has authorized me to surrender to your forces."

Incensed at this turn of affairs, the major, who wanted action and lots of it, turned to the interpreter and said, "Surrender, nothing. Tell that so-and-so to take that truckload of K rations over there and get back where he came from."

But there's one thing I do admire about the state where the men are men and the women are glad of it. Texans all admit we helped them win the war.

We worked for the 354th, P-51 Mustang, Fighter Group and took off from their air strip to do a show at Kaufbeuren for the 2nd Air Disarmament Wing and the 55th Fighter Group. They let us stand in the EM chowline for some great beef stew, tomatoes, beans, canned peaches, and cake. And when Colonna saw what I was putting away he said, "Hope, if you take on any more weight you'll look as fat as you are."

I won't say we did a bad show at Kaufbeuren, but eight Mustangs escorted us a couple of miles and played a game of Scrape Rivet with our C-47. We were cruising at about 180 m.p.h., but from the way those fighters whipped by, we could have been waiting for an order in a drive-in.

We did our next show at Fürstenfeldbruck, just west of Munich, for the 29th Tactical Air Command. And after the show we spent the night billeted with the men; that is, all but Gale, June, Patty, and Ruth. The USO had rules, you know. Dammit.

To civilians, all guys in uniform look alike, but each outfit has its outstanding personality. The OP of the 29th Tactical was a character from Brooklyn named Demetrios Sazani. He was a technical sergeant who once ran concessions at the Century of Progress in New York. And some said Sazani made more progress than the century.

He promoted everything around the base. Saturday nights he ran a bingo game for cognac and wine, with a grand prize of $300 in cash. He also managed one of the ETO's best softball teams. In his off hours, Sazani ran the EM and Officers' Club Dances, and it was rumored that you could coax him to oversee a crap game now and then. I'd hate to say he was doing better than okay financially in the Army. But he was the only sergeant anyone ever heard of who had a full colonel for an orderly.

The only show we did in Europe in battle helmets after V-E Day was in Eschwege for the 363d Photo Reconnaissance Group of the 5th Division. It looked like rain, so instead of our playing out-of-doors, they set up a stage for us in a big German hangar that had taken a couple of direct hits. Most of the roof was gone and what was left of the walls swayed

Deutschland unter Allies

gently in the breeze. Right over our heads a loose beam was juggling about two tons of very loose brick. For once in my life I didn't want to bring the house down. I was even afraid of one loud laugh. GI's were hanging from the roof, the rafters, and pipes.

Twice a couple of pipes pulled loose, and sections of wall and soldiers piled up in the aisles. It was the only time I ever had to duck flying bricks *before* I told the jokes.

At Fritzlar—no relation to Bert Lahr—we checked in with the 9th Air Tactical Command. While signing some shortsnorters a soldier handed me a five-dollar bill as big as a Stork Club menu with a picture of an Indian chief on it. I had an uncle who made better-looking money. It turned out the bill was the McCoy. It was issued in 1803, and the owner (who asked me not to mention his name because the Geneva Conference might misundertand) told me he liberated ten of the antique fives from a German SS trooper. Shows how long they'd been planning an invasion.

But what a welcome we got wherever we showed up! We made an emergency landing at Kassel. A PFC came rushing out onto the field and hollered, "Get that plane off the runway!"

I stuck my head out the escape hatch and said, "It's me, Bob Hope."

The guy took another look to make sure and then hollered, "Get that plane off the field!"

A few minutes later we heard a tremendous explosion and saw a big column of smoke rising not far away. It felt like a near miss, and I began to think V-E Day had been repealed. "What's going on?" I asked.

"You'll have to talk louder," the guy said. "I can't hear you."

So I took my head out of the gopher hole and asked him what all the shooting was for.

"No shooting," he said. "They just discovered a stack of 300 five-hundred-pound German bombs back in the woods and they're blowing them up."

After we got a parking permit for the plane, I, being the head of our unit, sent one of the girls up to explain that we'd been forced down and would have to have food and lodging till we could go on. The guy who told us to get off the field just handed her a little book and walked away. The book was called *Russian Infantry Tactics and How to Live off the Land*.

All of a sudden a Cleveland boy named Frank Cheek, who

Deutschland unter Allies

just happened to be a lieutenant in charge of the Officers' Club, came out and shook hands with us. "You're welcome to stay here with us," Lt. Cheek said, graciously.

"Great!" I said, "we'll do a show for you."

But they fed us, anyway. While we were eating, some of the men started to tell us about a thing called an atomic bomb that had been dropped on Hiroshima. It was a new thing. He said, "It doesn't blow up a city. It blows it down." They told us how the bomb just seemed to vaporize everything within a radius of two or three miles.

So This Is Peace

As it turned out, it practically vaporized the peace it accelerated. While everyone began to look on the A-Bomb as the greatest force for evil since Eve ate the apple, and while scientists pleaded that the world forget it as a weapon, the Army and Navy immediately went to work to perfect a counterweapon. The Army soon announced a defensive measure, the exact nature of which has not yet been disclosed. But the Anti-A-Bomb weapon is probably some simple little gadget that blows you together again after you've been blown to pieces by the A-Bomb. If it isn't, that's the line along which to work.

At Point Mugue and all over the deserts of southern California and Texas the Army and Navy are shooting rockets into the air, launching molten metal projectiles that will strike like a bolt of lightning, and testing all kinds of destructive devices that are so fantastic they make Colonna's mustache look conservative.

The Navy has even gone so far as to announce the nature of some of these new death dealers. For instance, they have a projectile that actually chases its target. Whether or not this can be applied to a ripe tomato, the Navy doesn't say. But it's certainly not a very nice thing for the Navy to do to actors after all we actors have done for the Navy. Or maybe that's what they have on their minds. Anyway, actors have given the Navy some of the best years of Henry Fonda and Robert Montgomery; to say nothing of Robert Taylor, Eddie Albert, and Victor Mature. Vic Mature was really in the Coast Guard, but that was only because a hunk of man like that has to spend a lot of time worrying whether the coast is clear.

The ordnance wizards are also working out flying bombs that will seek out the heat of factory districts in the center of

Deutschland unter Allies

comparatively cool residential areas. The hot spots will naturally be the targets. This makes it mandatory for countermeasures to be worked out at once to protect the homes of Hedy Lamarr and Paulette Goddard.

But I'm sure these will be found. After the lance and the sword came the shield and armor. And as soon as a better tank was perfected they called it *The Lost Weekend.* You see, I can still joke. I'm not worried at all about the fantastic home-wreckers of the future. Even the thought of germ warfare doesn't scare me. I feel that the way we're developing weapons to combat weapons, the time *must* come when everything will automatically cancel out everything else and we'll be right back to where one nation just hollers across the border to another nation, "Aw, my brudder's a cop!"

But even those combat troops we saw weren't really startled by the news of what the first A-Bomb did to Hiroshima. They had all seen what happened when Unit 676 hit a mess hall.

After leaving the mess and the mess hall in a mess, we were driven through town to see what the RAF had done in seventeen minutes. Kassel was pretty well knocked down. You could stand on tiptoe almost any place in the downtown section and see the whole city, which wasn't there.

Outside of town one of the ex-Kaiser's castles—his summer palace—was still standing. But the inside of the place looked exactly as if that guy Superman had gone through it with a vacuum cleaner. It makes me feel terrible to walk into a place and see *nothing* left. I like souvenirs, too.

I was pretty tired by the time we got back to the field. But I didn't sleep well. Before lying down I happened to pound the mattress with my fist and broke three knuckles.

So This Is Peace

We'd been on our way to Munich to do a broadcast when we were forced down at Kassel. But we finally made Munich about three in the afternoon, thinking our broadcast was scheduled for seven. What we found out was that they had an audience waiting at the Prinzregenten Theater for us. So we piled into some cars and rushed to the theater, trying to work out a few routines on the way. But what we put on could have brought back the crystal set.

The control booth at the theater turned out to be a broom closet full of captured German equipment and manned by

Deutschland unter Allies

Kraut engineers who didn't understand English. We went on the air before our baggage arrived, and Ruth Denas found she couldn't make an accordion out of matchboxes and Kleenex. On top of that, I told five jokes and the microphone went dead. Either those engineers were lying that they couldn't understand English, or it's the first time I was ever criticized by the electrical system.

Fortunately, Capt. Sandy Cummings, of the Armed Forces Network, helped us sweat it out. Sandy's uncle is Irving Cummings, who did what he could with what I had when he directed the Paramount picture, *Louisiana Purchase*. Those AFN guys did a swell job over there, both during and after the war, keeping the men happy, not only with transcriptions of American shows, but with little programs they dreamed up on the spur of the moment, like "Luncheon at München," "Bouncin' in Bavaria," "Midnight in Munich," and "Rhythm in the Reich."

Really nothing stopped those AFN boys. Sandy told me that once in Frankfurt they'd scheduled a concert by Glenn Miller's band. But they couldn't get the equipment to carry the music to the sending stations. So they plugged it into the local telephone system, and for an hour, when some *Hausfrau* called the butcher for wieners, she got "The Chattanooga Choo Choo."

After the broadcast, about 7:30 that evening, we did a show for about 25,000 men of the Third Army at a big athletic field. They were General Patton's men, and Old Blood and Guts' influence was immediately apparent. All Patton's troops were ordered to wear helmets. And they all did! Everyone knows how strict he was about spit and polish. Every GI seemed to have his own personal MP and there were three speed-limit signs for every car on the road. The saluting got so promiscuous they even saluted me. And while we were there, a rumor started that all enlisted men would have to salute passing aircraft because they were piloted by officers.

But kidding on the square, General George Patton, Jr., was one of the greatest military men this country ever had. His contribution to our victory was so enormous that whatever mistakes he made and whatever he might have said must be excused and forgotten in the over-all record.

Before leaving Munich we all went to the PX to draw our rations. We had regular GI ration cards which entitled us to seven packs of cigarettes, six bars of candy, two packs of gum, and a cake of soap a week. The clerk at the PX turned out to be a fellow alumnus of mine from Cleveland's Fairmont

Junior High School, Pvt. Mike Artate. So I got my favorite scent of soap. Mike told everyone they remembered me so well at Fairmont that they had my picture up with a caption under it saying, "Don't let this happen to you!"

From Munich we hopped up to Nuremberg for the GI Olympics. The town was really muscle-bound. Soldiers and sailors from all over the ETO filled Soldiers' Field, née the Nuremberg Stadium, battling each other on the cinders or cheering their favorites. It was one of the greatest days of my life, in spite of the fact that it was raining and everyone was too interested in the track events to ask me to say a few words. Here's why.

It was while watching the GI Olympic meet that they announced Japan had offered to surrender. The whole stadium full of guys seemed to rise twenty-five feet in the air. They cheered for thirty minutes. Pandemonium reigned, but by that time we were all so wet we didn't notice it. The only thing that could have capped that climax would have been for the sun to come out and a rainbow to stretch across the sky. That's what will happen when C. B. de Mille makes a picture of it.

But even C. B. couldn't improve on the noise those Yanks made, cheering for victory in a spot where only a few months before Hitler raised his regular *Heil!*

And what was most wonderful of all . . . not one of those soldiers or sailors showed the slightest disappointment at the news that their trip to the Orient would probably be canceled.

The rain had killed all chances of doing the big show we had scheduled for that evening in the stadium, so we did two little shows at the opera house. The only difference was that the opera-house roof was so full of holes you got soaked with filtered water. The audience couldn't really applaud but they splashed loudly.

Nuremberg got hit very badly, you know. Experts tell me the only thing comparable to the way Nuremberg was flattened would be any city in the United States after an American Legion Convention.

The GI Olympics attracted a lot of "types" to the area. "Type," that's the French version of our word character, meaning the unique denizen of show business and Broadway who made a rich man out of Damon Runyon. The watchword of these Broadway Boys in the Army was, "Don't knock the street." And when they gathered in my room, it could have passed for one of the smaller tables at Lindy's.

The hecklers included Sgt. Jimmy Cannon and Pvt. Dave Gordon of *Stars and Stripes*; Corp. Billy Conn, who was a champion for thirteen rounds; Allan Jackson, the INS man (that's a news syndicate, not a branch of the Army); Sgt. Harold Grey; Colonel Swede Larson, ex-Navy football coach, then in the Marines; and Major Torchy Torrance, also of the Marines, who was at the meet with an eye to promoting a similar one in the Pacific Theater.

This little meeting took place in my room at the Grand Hotel, which was reserved for Hitler's private use two months a year. He wouldn't have known the old place. The RAF moved the lobby four blocks east and most of the rooms were sports models with convertible walls. Mine was the only room I'd ever lived in that had north, east, south, and west exposures. And I didn't need a key because there wasn't any door. There was a nice roof, though, and twenty-four hours a day two of the stronger PW's held up the outside corner. This is a nice kind of place to live in on a rainy night.

It was still raining the next day when we showed up at Salzburg, the spot where all the long-haired musicians used to spend their summer vacations loading up on the three B's: Beethoven, Blutwurst, and Beer.

We raced out to a hillside where they'd scheduled our show, and there were 12,000 guys of the famous Rainbow Division waiting for the rainbow. It's always that way with GI audiences. The Germans and Japs couldn't stop them and they won't let a little rain do it, either.

It was really so wet that Patty Thomas' dance turned into a sort of aquacade ballet. But just to show that good things come to good people, in about fifteen minutes the rain let up.

So This Is Peace

Two hours later our shoes stopped squishing.

Salzburg's really a colorful little town, and unlike most of the spots we'd hit, it hadn't been. The natives were still walking around the streets as if they were looking for a masquerade party. They wear *Lederhosen,* which are leather shorts, with those Lanz of Salzburg suspenders. The men also wear those peaked Alpine caps with a whisk broom stuck in the back. Billy Conn said it was wonderful to see a local wolf bend over to kiss the hand of a *Fräulein* and brush her teeth at the same time.

CHAPTER 10

To the Victors Belong the Spoiled

WE PICKED up Billy Conn at Mannheim, formerly a city. Shortly after we landed on the 27th Fighter Group's air strip we lost Patty Thomas. Billy Conn was her replacement. Billy Conn for Patty Thomas. Those two, side by side, could have given Slim Gaillard the idea for "Cement Mixer, Putti, Putti."

But Patty had been having wisdom-tooth trouble. Come to think of it, she's the second tap dancer in this book to have trouble with her back teeth. Maybe they jar them out of line. It's possible. There's something about Patty that made *me* get out of line. But she put me right back in my place.

Anyway, we finally convinced her to check into a hospital and have the tooth attended to. She agreed when MP's began stopping her to see what she was smuggling in her mouth. It was shortly after this that we ran into Billy and inducted him into Unit 676. I billed him as "the guy Joe Louis stayed thirteen rounds with in 1941." Not long after that Uncle Sam started looking for fighters and engaged both Billy and Joe.

Billy'd been overseas a year and a half when we ran into him, traveling with a Special Service Sports Unit. When we annexed him to our little group, by courtesy of General Strawbridge, his CO was Horton Smith, the golfer. Smith was a captain then and some say he had a caddie to carry his double bars. Also in the unit were George Lott and Tom Harmon, the tennis sharks; Bill Cavanaugh, the West Point boxing instructor; Fred Frankhouse, of baseball; Chick Harbert, another golfer; Saul Schiff, the ping-pong champ; and Billy's opponent in his exhibition matches, his little brother, Jackie. If that outfit had ever gone up against some of the German Schnapps, a lot of muscle would have gotten stiff.

But we took Billy out of the rough-house environment of sports and got him started telling jokes with us. And I must say he showed a lot of courage. But then he's only been knocked out by two people ... Joe Louis and his father-in-law.

Billy told us a story about weighing in at Madison Square Garden for a big National War Fund relief bout that never took place. General Surles and a fine collection of Army and Navy brass were watching the weighing-in ceremony and rubbing their hands over the loot the War Fund was going to get from this big exhibition match.

The boys listened as they cut it up among themselves ... $200,000 for Army Relief ... $200,000 for Navy Relief ... $100,000 for the Marine Corps ... $100,000 for the Coast

To the Victors Belong the Spoiled

Guard ... the WAC was getting some ... the Waves ... the Spars ... everyone was being handed a hunk of the expected take. Everyone, that is, except the two boys who were weighing in. They had no claim. They were both soldiers under orders. But it was tough to listen to. So finally Billy leaned over and whispered, "Say, Joe, get a load of those guys cutting up our gate. What do *we* get out of this fight?"

Joe put his hand over Billy's mouth and whispered, "Not so loud, boy. If that general with the four stars hears you, they'll send you so far it'll take an eight-cent postcard to reach you."

What a wonderful guy Louis is ... and what a fine soldier he was! The country honored him with its highest noncombatant award—the Legion of Merit.

As for Billy, flying is the only thing I know that can scare him. Whenever our troupe got into the air, Billy got out his rosary. And when the weather curdled and we had to go on instruments, Billy went on beads. One of the things I'm most proud to own as a souvenir of our last trip to Europe is the string of beads Billy Conn gave me.

The night Billy and Joe met over the heavyweight championship for the third time, I'm sure everyone remembered what a game battle Billy'd put up in his first two meetings with Joe. I remembered, too. And I recalled saying to Louis the first time I met him, which was just after the second Conn fight, "Joe, you cost me a lot of money. I bet on Conn twice and I lost. And I bet on Nova and I lost."

Joe just smiled, winked, and said, "We'll get it back next time."

In spite of this I don't think either man went into that championship fight with any cocksure feeling of victory. By either man I mean Billy and me. Joe, I know, had plenty of confidence in his ability to handle himself. And practically called the round he chose to leave after.

There was a story just before the fight that someone warned Joe, "Look out for Billy. He may try to tire you out by running away from you. Don't let him run away from you."

Joe just said, "He can run but he can't hide."

And Joe proved this in the eighth round. Billy's backers say he could have come out for the ninth. But by that time Joe was dressed and on his way to a midnight movie. Joe finished the fight without one drop of perspiration on him. Billy got just one drop. Actually Billy suffered from the same trouble all of Joe's repeat opponents suffer from . . . memory of a murderous punch.

Only we fighters who have been in the ring, throwing leather, know what it's like to take those lethal punches. Or didn't you know I had a career as a professional fighter before I found out there was an easier way to make a living? Like Maxie Rosenbloom, Max Baer, and Freddie Steele, Billy may decide to become an actor. Most fighters do, if they can. I know. I tried.

I still don't know why all the fuss was made just because the two boys touched gloves at the beginning of the eighth round. They're supposed to touch gloves at the beginning of the last round . . . and that was the last round. The way I heard it on my radio, the bell started the eighth . . . Billy's glove touched Joe's glove . . . Joe's glove touched Billy's chin . . . Billy's chin touched the canvas, and I know what kind of touch that is. I finished my career as a professional fighter that way, too.

We were playing New Orleans City Park Stadium on June 19, the night of the fight. So at fight time I stopped the show and told the folks we'd tune in the big battle. "You know," I explained, "a little financial interest. If Louis wins, I'm back in vaudeville."

Between rounds I told my audience how I knew Billy personally and gave them a complete rundown on how the fight was going. At the end of the first round I told them it was just the way we planned it.

At the end of the second round I said, "Just tactic."

When the third round finished, I said. "Now we're tiring him."

At the finish of the fourth I had things going just as planned. By the fifth, Louis was falling into our trap. By the sixth everything looked great. At the end of the seventh I said, "It won't be long now."

And that was the only time I was right. At the end of the eighth I said, "Well! Money isn't everything." But sometimes I wonder about that.

So This Is Peace

It was the first fight in history with the regulation-size ring and ten thousand ringside seats . . . ten thousand ringside seats at one hundred dollars a squat. In fact, the prices were scaled so high all the way down the line that only about fifty thousand people showed up. This is a lot of folks. But there was room in the Yankee Stadium for at least twenty thousand more.

Poor Uncle Mike Jacobs only grabbed himself a gate of about two million bucks. He said he was very disappointed. He expected three million. Never before were so few disappointed by so much.

However, in spite of the fact that Billy had as much explaining to do after the fight as the average unwed mother, I'd say both he and Joe had an extremely profitable evening. And all the Great Waltz proved was that Joe Louis was still the best fighter the country ever developed and Billy wasn't.

It's a shame that all men who were in the service didn't find it as easy to reconvert to civilian life as those two men did.

I walked into a bank the other day and saw a former ensign at work. I knew he was an ensign the minute I saw the narrow gold stripe around his mop handle. But I don't blame the men; they have a lot of readjusting to do. A guy who'd been a member of a B-29 crew for two years finally went back to soda jerking. But before he could put a cherry on top of a banana split, he had to climb into the chandelier and holler, "Bombs away!" His big trouble was that after Ray Milland made *The Lost Weekend*, it was so crowded in the chandelier. Another B-29 guy who now drives a cab just by force of habit takes all fares—no matter where they want to go—by way of Tokyo. I'll know peace is really here to stay when I step into a cab and the driver takes me where *I* want to go.

To the Victors Belong the Spoiled

A colonel in the Air Force got himself a chicken farm, after reading Betty MacDonald's biography of me, *The Egg and I*, but every morning before he'll let the chickens start laying their eggs, the colonel goes into the coop and starts to brief them. By force of habit, airmen don't use elevators; they just bail out down the shaft.

A kid from a farm in Ohio who'd been a Navy tail gunner for three years went back to work milking, and the first morning the cow turned around and hollered, "Hey, take it easy! Those aren't triggers, you know!" This boy really had been indoctrinated into Navy ways. The day some of his buddies came to visit the farm, he fed the cow talcum powder so he'd be able to serve the boys powdered milk.

But many of the men benefit by their service training. An ex-ball-turret gunner is now in Skinnay Ennis' band. He's not such a good musician, but he's a big attraction. Very few people have ever seen a bass fiddler who plays from the inside.

Of course, the mechanics aren't having much trouble. The Army and Navy air forces and ground forces gave them such wonderful training that it doesn't take any time at all for them to fix a car. There's one of those ex-Air Force men in the North Hollywood garage where I take my car. He did a great job, only when I shift into third the wheels come up and fold into the fenders.

Electronics and radar is another field of service training that's given many a man a head start in civilian life. One Navy technician leads a happy civilian life today because of his knowledge of radar. It's made it possible for him to be out of the house three hours before his mother-in-law arrives.

Another ex-Army man who stepped right into a fine job in civilian life, as a result of his Army training, was a top sergeant I met in Germany. He got himself a very responsible position . . . souring pickles for the Heinz Company.

There was even a lot of talk and discussion about how I would reconvert from war to peace. Wherever I went after V-J Day one question was constantly being asked: "What will Bob Hope do now?" I was asking it. And you'd be surprised how many people told me what I could do.

Of course I'm only kidding. Like everybody else I had my postwar plans. I used to lie awake nights just dreaming about one of those shiny new kitchens where the stove looks like the sink and the sink looks like your wife's mother. And I had even worse dreams.

Sometimes I dreamed that they included me among the war criminals. There *were* people who saw my shows who questioned which side I was on. But I wasn't really worried. I figured I could always plead insanity. The trouble was I knew they'd believe me.

Actually, I guess the same thoughts that were running through the head of every GI were running through my head. Only, of course, in my head they had more room to

To the Victors Belong the Spoiled

run. In common with the GI's I kept thinking of a nice long rest. The only difference was that the GI's really wanted one and I was afraid I'd be given one.

But until V-J Day I went happily about my work in Europe. I was secretly looking for Hitler. I wanted to ask him how he got where he did, with a face like his, without getting laughs. You can't look for Hitler without going to Berchtesgaden. So one morning we headed for there in a rainstorm, traveling in a couple of sieve-topped recon. cars.

A narrow winding road outside the town of Berchtesgaden led to Hitler's little subdivision. He had quite a settlement there in the hills. Besides his own modest little lean-to there was Göring's house, Martin Bormann's place, several large barracks for SS guards, the Plättehof, where minor Nazi officials used to be entertained, and a sort of combination hothouse and nursery where SS babies were bred and trained

So This Is Peace

from infancy to be personal bodyguards to the Führer. Just thinking of those little sons of Berchtesgaden being brought up from babyhood as SS troopers turns my stomach.

Of course, there used to be a big swimming pool by courtesy of Der Führer in connection with all those buildings, but by the time I arrived, there were three by courtesy of the RAF. The whole place was pretty well beat up, but the hotel was still in one piece, so we stopped there and ran into PFC Teddy Zablidowsky, from Manhattan, whose uncle used to run the Nordic Athletic Club, where I did many a benefit while on Broadway.

Teddy was a member of B Battery, 441st AAA Battalion, stationed there, and offered to show us around. We climbed through the debris in Hitler's living room and tramped around some of the twenty miles of tunnels that are under the area. Those tunnels were so well equipped they even had a beauty parlor. I wanted to stop, but the operator was off duty.

After we came to the surface we got back in our leaky cars and drove up a winding one-way road scratched into the side of Mt. Kehlstein. What curves! The guy who designed that road must have been working from a blueprint of Betty Grable.

The cars kept leaking and pretty soon our USO pants looked like those Salzburg shorts.

Finally we got to the top, parked the cars, and walked into another tunnel which took us a few hundred feet into the mountain to Hitler's private elevator. We rode up with his personal operator. The elevator had two levels, with a sort of basement reached through a trap door where his SS guards rode.

The construction of this little shack of Adolf's, including

To the Victors Belong the Spoiled

the Eagle's Nest on top, is said to have required three years and the labor of 3000 slave workmen. And although the day I was there the visibility wasn't more than three inches, Hitler was supposed to have been able to see three countries from his Eagle's Nest. Too bad he couldn't see the United States.

Some say his eyes were bigger than his armies.

The day I was there Hitler's E. N. was filled with Uncle Samuel's EM and one of the most interesting sights of the day was a big crap game on Hitler's conference table. I left the conference early. What happened to me should have happened to Hitler earlier.

But I managed to borrow a little money from General Ladd, whom I'd met in Alaska. He didn't mind lending me money. He was used to it. General Ladd was commanding the 9th Division, a bunch of guys I'd played for in Africa. We did a show for them to cancel the debt. And after the show we went over to the Notorious Red Cross Club. Notorious is not an adjective, it's the 9th Division code word. Ruth Denas and June Bruner helped keep the whole town of Ingolstadt awake that night with a jam session. It was quite an occasion. Kay Limoges, of Rockford, Ill., who'd had fourteen months overseas, had just opened the club and was holding a celebration to commemorate the construction of the 100,000th doughnut. Patty Thomas, who had rejoined 676, officiated at the dunking.

Among others present were Red Howell, a former jockey who rode for Bing, and Joe E. Brown. Red said he couldn't wait to get back up on some of Crosby's nags, as he needed the rest. I told him they now made Bing's steeds wear license plates so the judges could tell what year they started.

The next day, to remind me of the money I'd borrowed,

So This Is Peace

General Ladd invited me to lunch. Lunching with anyone you owe money to makes for dull conversation. But lunching with a soldier of the Occupation Army—brass or any GI—the conversation was exactly the same. He said, "How are things back in the States?" I took it from there.

I told him that everything looked promising. But by now he realizes as well as I do that we're all still waiting for those promises to be fulfilled. And many a GI's undoubtedly wondering what he's getting as a civilian in 1946 that he wasn't getting as a soldier in 1945. And that includes a kicking around.

You can almost take it step by step. One of the most universal gripes of the GI was living in barracks with a lot of other soldiers. So he came home and found himself living in an overcrowded house, or apartment, in an overcrowded neighborhood with relatives who weren't even as congenial as his buddies in the barracks because his buddies weren't sacrificing any of their comforts for him.

He didn't have any source of income, which he had in the Army (such as it was), and when he went to buy anything he ran into the same kind of avarice he learned to deal with on a GI basis. He found a guy still had "to have a friend" to get something. Actually, the only thing that changed in his life when he changed his suit was that the superior officer was no longer always around flaunting his superiority.

The one thing he managed to duck was a gee pulling rank. But in his heart of hearts he didn't find any essential difference between the insulting attitude of people with services and goods for sale and a really chicken shavetail. In spite of all this, however, I guess an ex-serviceman should feel satisfied. He accomplished his mission.

For three years he stood in line to preserve a way of life.

To the Victors Belong the Spoiled

He stood in line to draw his clothes, to get his chow, to get his medical attention, to get his entertainment. So now, as a civilian, he can stand in line to buy his clothes, to buy his food, to see a doctor, and to see a movie. Only now as he stands in line he's not so sure he'll get what he's queued up for and, if he gets it, he'll have to pay for it. But he *has* maintained a way of life. Only it's the way of life he learned to dislike while fighting for the one he liked. It's not very surprising that everybody's a little uncertain, confused, and upset.

Fortunately, there was no way of foreseeing this, that day at lunch with General Ladd. So we just had a nice lunch and drove to Regensburg, where we went directly to the Bischofshof, now a hotel, which had been originally built in the tenth century and looked to me like a long description in a short story by Ludwig Bemelmans. We unloaded our bags and hit right out for a beautiful Austrian cow pasture where we did a show for the men of the Third Army's XIIth Corps and five cows. That was one show where we had mooed music. We had a little trouble with the PA system, though. And finally discovered that a guy who was sitting right in front of the horn thought it was too loud and stuffed his shirt in it. Lots of people have told me my jokes were strained, but never through laundry.

And one look at that guy's shirt explained why the gags all sounded dirty.

When Unit 676 moved on to Passau the Krauts must have thought the 8th Air Force was attacking again. We arrived in eight planes. They were Piper Cubs, or what the Army calls 1-4's. They can just barely carry one passenger. I'd put on so much weight with that German beer, they had to make two trips to haul me. But I finally arrived at the Gasthaus.

So This Is Peace

Those little Cubs cruise about seventy-five, and if you've never seen one you'd swear they're something an ambitious boy scout whipped up out of an old washing-machine motor, a clothes pole, and a few yards of bedding. We'd ridden in them in the Pacific, and this time my pilot was Lt. Doyle Davis of Waco, Texas, and the 183rd Observation Group.

During the war those guys cruised over the front, spotting targets for artillery, and they're really risky fliers. Any one of them who's caught flying over a telephone wire is considered a sissy. I won't say they fly too low, but twice hedges hopped us. And they buzz everything, civilians, cows, wagons, jeeps . . . they do more buzzing than Lana Turner's doorbell.

Some of the other travelers at the Gasthaus were Cpl. Milton Charleston, who used to work with Ken Murray and Olsen and Johnson, and Sandy McPherson, a Scotch comic who used to be with Gus Edwards. Both these boys were doing a swell job with a GI show called *Foxhole Frolics* which was playing the area. But we did *our* show just the same in the Passau Sportplatz for men of the 102nd Division and the 83rd (Thunderbolt) Division, which reached the Elbe beachhead, thus becoming the unit nearest Berlin on V-E Day.

Around Passau, as at every place else I touched in Germany in the summer of 1945, the talk was about where Hitler was.

I heard one guy from the 83rd say to another, "I wonder if Hitler's happy in Palestine."

Before leaving for Pilsen, we visited an ancient stone castle at Passau that was so old they'd actually made their final FHA payment.

And it was almost as picturesque and romantic-looking as a Hollywood drive-in. This castle, the Oberhaus, was used

To the Victors Belong the Spoiled

for a rest center for the men of the 83rd Division. It was a great spot for an infantryman to relax. There was a Terrace Beer Garden overlooking the Danube, which, at that point, unless I'm color-blind, is green; a library; a theater, with three pictures a day; a huge swimming pool; tennis courts; and off limits for officers.

We were still traveling in Piper Cubs when we landed in Czechoslovakia and did our show in the center of Pilsen's town square. It was wonderful to hear the MP's telling GI's that Bob Hope was on the square.

There were about ten thousand men there from XXIInd Corps HQ, the 8th and 16th Armored Divisions, the 503rd Medical Battalion, and the 102nd Cavalry Group. Besides all these GI's, about half the cast of Pilsen turned out to case our act and try to figure what we were peddling. I think they finally decided we were some new type of displaced person.

But I suppose I shouldn't have been surprised that the people were confused by what we were trying to do. Only a few weeks before, Jack Benny had been through and played his violin for them. What a thing to do to a people who love music the way Czechoslovakians do! But then Larry Adler was along with his harmonica. And Martha Tilton sang. And Ingrid Bergman. That's all. Just Ingrid Bergman. None of the GI's seemed to remember what she did. They just looked misty-eyed and murmured her name.

In Czechoslovakia, as in France, we noted the difference between Germany and the once German-occupied countries. The children looked different. In the ex-occupied countries the kids were always skinny and war-faded, their clothing tattered and patched. The German kids got fed.

We lived in Pilsen at the Hotel Skoda, and I must say I got wonderful service. The first morning I was late waking up, but Lt. Dean Sweet, of Springfield, Ill., who ran the place, personally got me out of bed, with the help of a pitcher of ice water. I had to spend the whole morning thinking about Hedy Lamarr to get my goose pimples to go back.

We did a show in Vimperk in the Sudetenland, too. That's the province Hitler marched into to protect the Germans living there. When we marched in, they were being protected by the men of the 94th Division, the guys who cracked the Siegfried Line and were called, by the Wehrmacht, "Roosevelt's Butchers."

It seemed to me almost fatalistic that in this same "Butchers" Division I should run across my nephew Henry, as the slicing of ham in more ways than one has long been a Hope family attribute. When I first saw him standing there in his lieutenant's uniform, with the silver star on his tunic, it seemed hard to believe that he was really a Hope. But later that night, when after a double Martini he tried to tell his colonel how the colonel had botched up an Elbe River crossing, I knew that he was a Hope, all right.

We did a show for a bunch of these men and then went on

To the Victors Belong the Spoiled

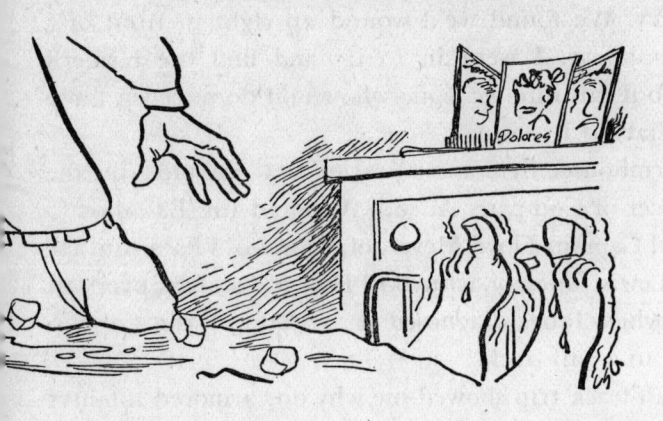

to Strakoniçe, had some lunch at the EM Mess and did another show for the balance of the 94th at McClune Field, a ball park outside of town.

The main occupation of the occupation troops in that area was making up rumors about when they'd go home. Every guy had his own personal rumor and would knock out the teeth of anyone else who tried to spread it. And those boys could certainly spread it. They were really imaginative. Pvt. Danny Willhite, of Detroit, told me he sent one of his rumors to a New York theatrical producer who cast it and it ran on Broadway for four months.

After our last show, we moved on in captured German command cars. Those German automobiles run like a cross between an old-fashioned coffee grinder and a rebuilt 1917 Stutz. They give out with more knocks than George Jean Nathan and did more to sabotage German Army transportation than the French underground.

Our little deal chugged along pitifully for about thirty miles, until we'd lost the rest of our convoy, then the lights went out, the motor went out, and we got out. But we were really lucky. We found we'd wound up right in front of a Czech farmhouse. I went in to try and find the farmer's daughter but ran into someone who could do me even more good— What am I writing?

The farmhouse, by some miracle, was occupied by the motor officer of Company A, 58th Armored Inf. Battalion, a guy named Captain Floyd Meyer, of Shawano, Wisconsin. He had T/4 Lewis Jones, of Schuylkill Haven, Pa., look over our rig. And when Jones diagnosed it as "kaput," the Captain sent us on in a half-track.

That half-track trip showed me why our armored infantry was so unbeatable. Nothing could stop them. After riding for an hour in one of those half-tracks, they were so numb they couldn't feel a bullet even if it hit 'em.

Thus we got to Heidelberg, where we did a show for the 324th, a wonderful bunch of about 25,000 men from 100th Division, 789th AAA Battalion and VIth Corps HQ. Their PRO was Lt. Ken Morgan, formerly of the *Hollywood Reporter*.

After another show for the 422nd, 980th, and 690th Field Artillery Battalions, Cpl. George Reise, of Des Moines, came on stage and presented Ruth, June, Patty, and Gale with a three-foot basket of flowers. It was a touching tribute but it caused a lot of trouble getting it home in our jeep.

Heidelberg had been declared an open city when a few artillery shells happened to drop in for pot luck, so it was in fair shape. I immediately checked in at the Schloss Hotel, where Mark Twain once stayed and did a lot of *his* writing. I even had Mark Twain's room. I'm sure because it had a picture of him on the walls, autographed, "From M. T. to Warner Brothers." It might have been a fake, though. It didn't look anything like Fredric March.

To the Victors Belong the Spoiled

It was one A.M. in Heidelberg when we got the wonderful news of V-J Day. One of the most historic days in the history of the world; certainly the most memorable day in my life.

We'd just finished two evening shows at the Heidelberg Capitol Theater for the Seventh Army HQ and 84th Division boys, and I was playing ping-pong with PFC Stanley Weise in our billet at the Schloss Hotel, when PFC Bonner F. Jennings, of Washington, D. C., suddenly burst in hollering, "It's finished! The war's over!"

Gale Robbins, whose husband was with the Air Force in the Pacific, gave out the first scream. Weise, whom the boys called "Brooklyn," just laid his paddle down and said softly, "Now I can go back to God's country, Flatbush."

Sgt. Pete Rozinski, of Duryea, Pennsylvania, and Sgt. Aldo DeAntoni, of Chicago, started pounding each other on the back.

Lt. Col. Donald L. Durfee turned to Lt. Lloyd Martin, of Seneca, S. C., and said, "Well, Lloyd, it looks like we'll be out of work soon." A hollow joke that sounded, even then, like grim words that I prayed would never become too true.

T/4 Mike Dohmen, our sound technician from Humphrey, Nebraska, took out some dog-eared pictures and started looking at them happily. Mike had a three-and-a-half-year-old kid in the States he'd never seen.

1st Lt. James Gillman, of East Bank, West Virginia, ran out of the room and came back with a bottle of real bonded bourbon. "I've been saving this till I made sure," he said gravely, and started pouring drinks.

That's about all. It didn't add up to much gaiety. When it was boiled down, the collective response to the news that the greatest war in history had ended in victory was more of a sigh than a cheer.

After three years, eight months, and seven days, we were at peace. Men began to make plans again as the realization came slowly that the world was truly won . . . and prayers grew fervent for the wisdom never again to lose it.

THE END

P.S.

Well, that's it.... Peace and a few of the events leading up to it. If some of it sounds dizzy, it's only because I wrote it while following my nose. And even when I stopped to write, it wasn't easy. With these new postwar pens, you either have to live under water, 20,000 feet in the air, or a lifetime.

And a lifetime's about what it would have taken not so very long ago to see as much of our United States as I saw in less than a month on our first personal-appearance tour for civilians.

We played in twenty-two different states in twenty-eight days. And I talked to a lot of civilians and ex-GI's in every section of the country. They all asked me just one thing. I got the same question from everyone, "Where's Bing?"

So This Is Peace

Yes, sir, I left Hollywood thinking this country was seething with internal confusion. People told me the conflicting interests of a nation the size of ours had finally gotten out of hand. But I soon discovered that the people in the Northwest, the people in the Southwest, the people in the Middle West, and the people in the Northeast and Southeast were all aching for exactly the same thing. They didn't want Utopia. They didn't expect any solo on the horn of plenty. All they wanted . . . all they were looking for . . . was a vacant house.

And they're all going to get them. The building boom has really started. Every place we went we saw new houses half built and happy families living in them.

But to take it up a tone: There's an endless string of new things coming along and old things growing more mellow just as there has always been and always will be. Even when the early colonists had the thought that all men are created equal, it was laughed at as a crazy postwar idea that wouldn't work. It worked. And it'll continue to work. It's still working better here, where it started, than any place else in the world. And while to some the postwar world might have seemed a little slow in getting started, take it from a traveler who's seen a lot of it . . . it hasn't been left at the post.

P.P.S.

The last word on the United Nations is found in the attack Tito's air force made on one of our unarmed C-47's to protect the sovereignty of little Yugoslavia. It's agreed that the United Nations was organized to protect small nations against big ones. But no one knows who protects the big ones from the little ones.

It seems the Security Council, without a police force, can't offer much security or give any very convincing counsel.

N.B.

What we have to admit is this. As it stands now, UN is just a beginning. But it's the beginning of UNdetermined ... UNsure ... and UNwilling.

APPENDIX NO. ONE

Joe Stalin dropped Litvinov from his diplomatic line-up in spite of the fact that Maxim knew how to play Western ball. Russo-Anglo-American relations immediately hit a new low. And the big double play of the 1946 diplomatic season was Bevin to Byrnes to Aspirin.

APPENDIX NO. TWO

Petrillo's Local No. 802 got itself locked out of a lot of hotels for asking for more money. This is a big switch. Musicians have been locked out of hotels before. But it was always the *hotel* that wanted the money.

EPILOGUE

Let's not let the word Peace get to mean a period of confusion between two wars.

BIBLIOGRAPHY

The author wishes to acknowledge the following books, pamphlets, and periodicals used in this work and recommends them for those who care to pursue the subject further:

So This Is Peace

- I Never Left Home, by Bob Hope (Simon and Schuster, pamphlet edition: $1.00)
- I Never Left the Bank, by Bing Crosby (Bank of America House Organ)
- The Rover Boys at Bastogne
- On a Slow Train Through Arkansas, by Thomas W. Jackson
- You Too Can Write, by Kathleen Winsor
- Little Black Sambo
- Legal Aspects of Moving-Picture Contracts, by Gang, Kopp & Tyre
- Encyclopaedia Britannica—Volume BRE-CHI
- Tom Swift and His Printing Machine
- Biennial Report on Use of Penicillin for Ulcers, by Mayo Brothers
- McGuffey's First Reader
- Memoirs of Hepcat County, by Gene Krupa
- The Hucksters, by Frederic Wakeman
- Alcoholics Anonymous
- Dope Habit Cured at Home, by #237651, Ossining, N. Y.
- We Never Lost a Battle, by Warner Brothers
- I Never Left Home, by Bob Hope (Simon and Schuster, cloth edition: $2.00)

ABOUT THE AUTHOR

Mr. Hope is a sports magnate. He recently acquired part ownership in the Cleveland Indians, who were, up to that point, a baseball team. This deal was consummated because of a lifelong desire of Mr. Hope's to get to first base at something.

Mr. Hope has also done radio and movie work.